Caroline Righton's

CREATE IT WITH PAINT IN AN EVENING

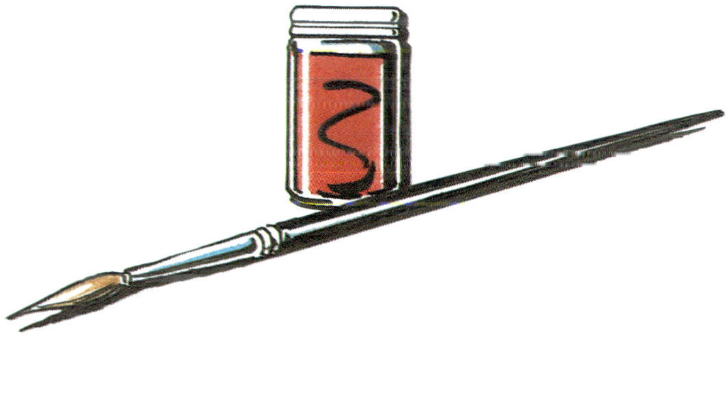

NEXUS SPECIAL INTERESTS

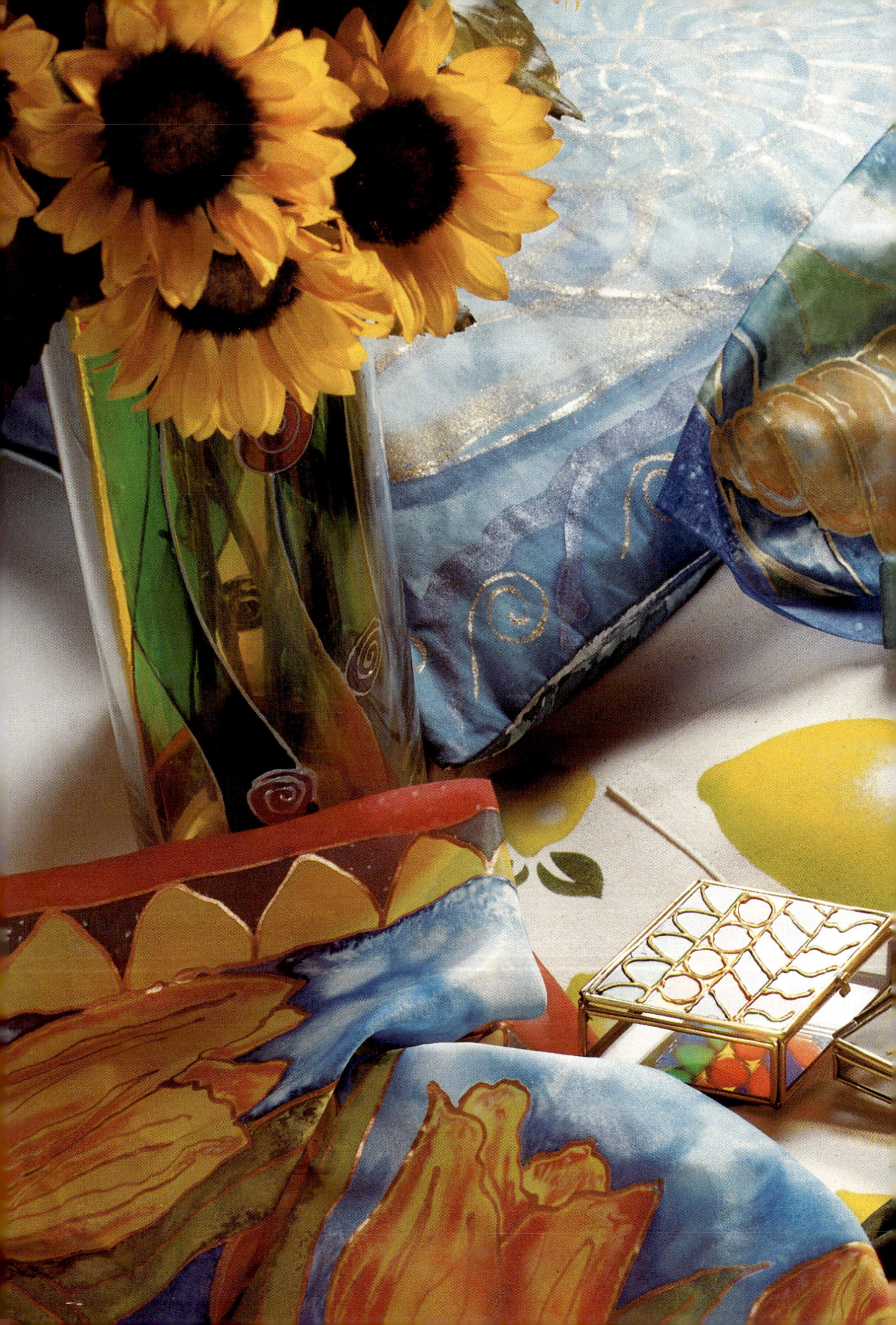

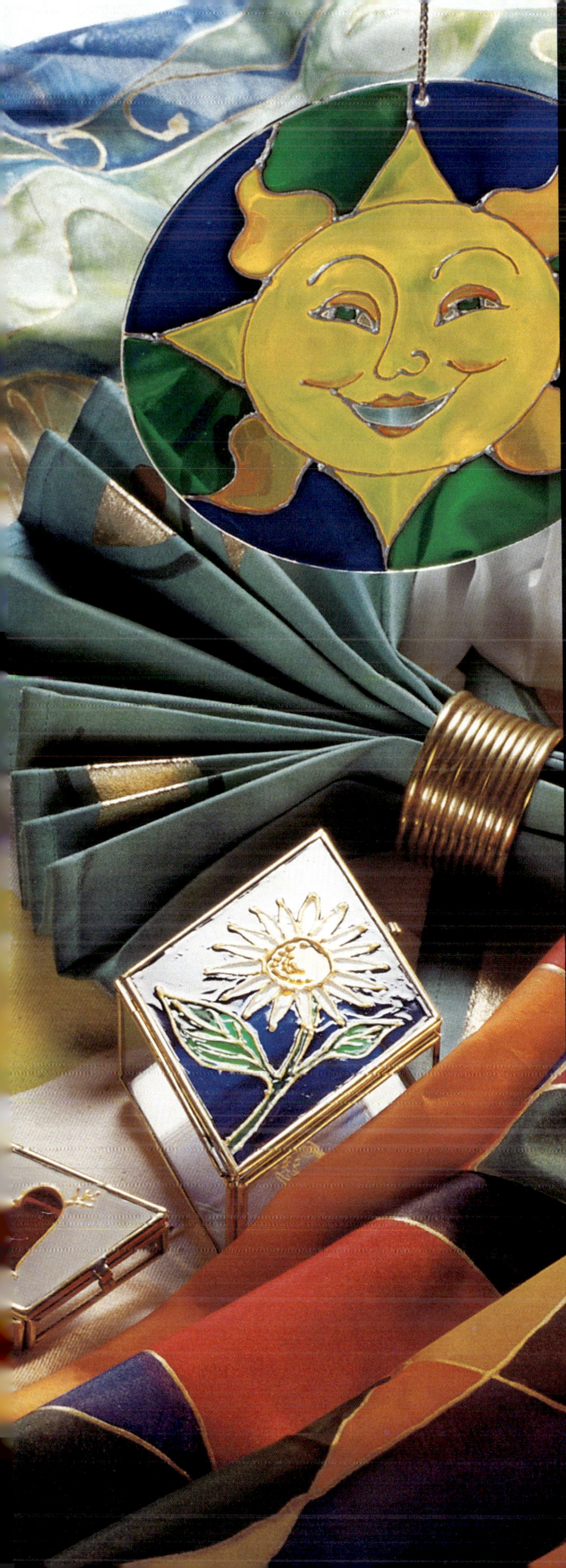

Caroline Righton's

CREATE IT WITH PAINT IN AN EVENING

DESIGNER
ELAINE DONOVAN

PHOTOGRAPHER
RICHARD LAING

NEXUS SPECIAL INTERESTS

Nexus Special Interests Ltd.
Nexus House
Boundary Way
Hemel Hempstead
Hertfordshire HP2 7ST
England

First published in Great Britain by Nexus Special Interests Ltd., 1998

ISBN 1-85486-174-3

Dedicated to Dad, Mark and Bob

Colour separations by PDQ, Bungay, Suffolk
Printed and bound in Great Britain by Jarrold Book Printing, Thetford, Norfolk

CONTENTS

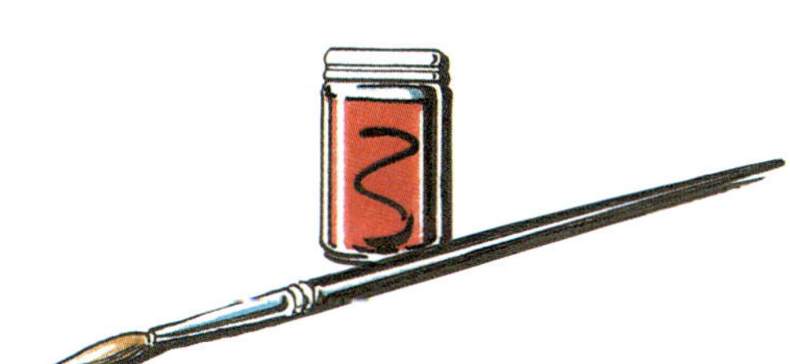

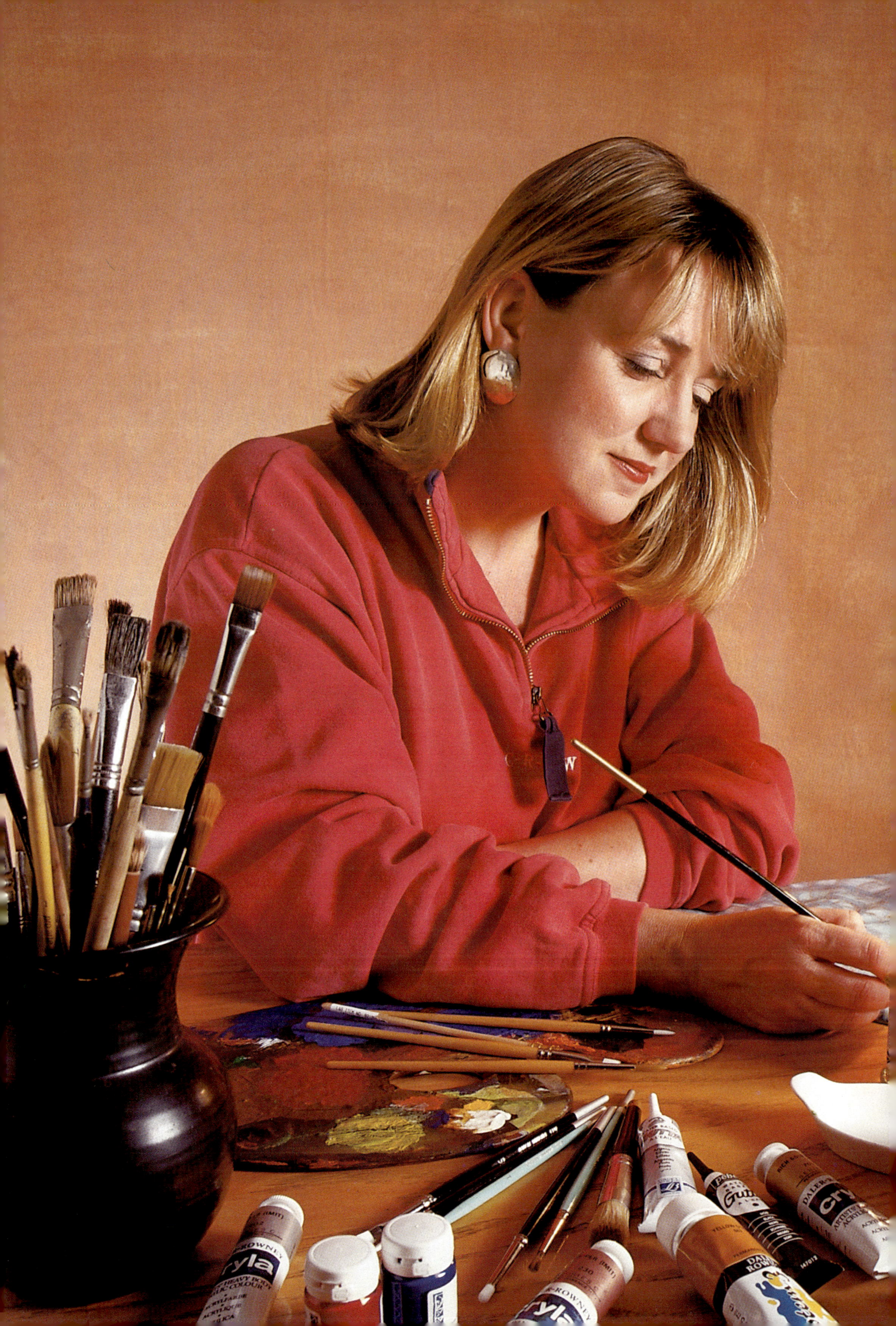

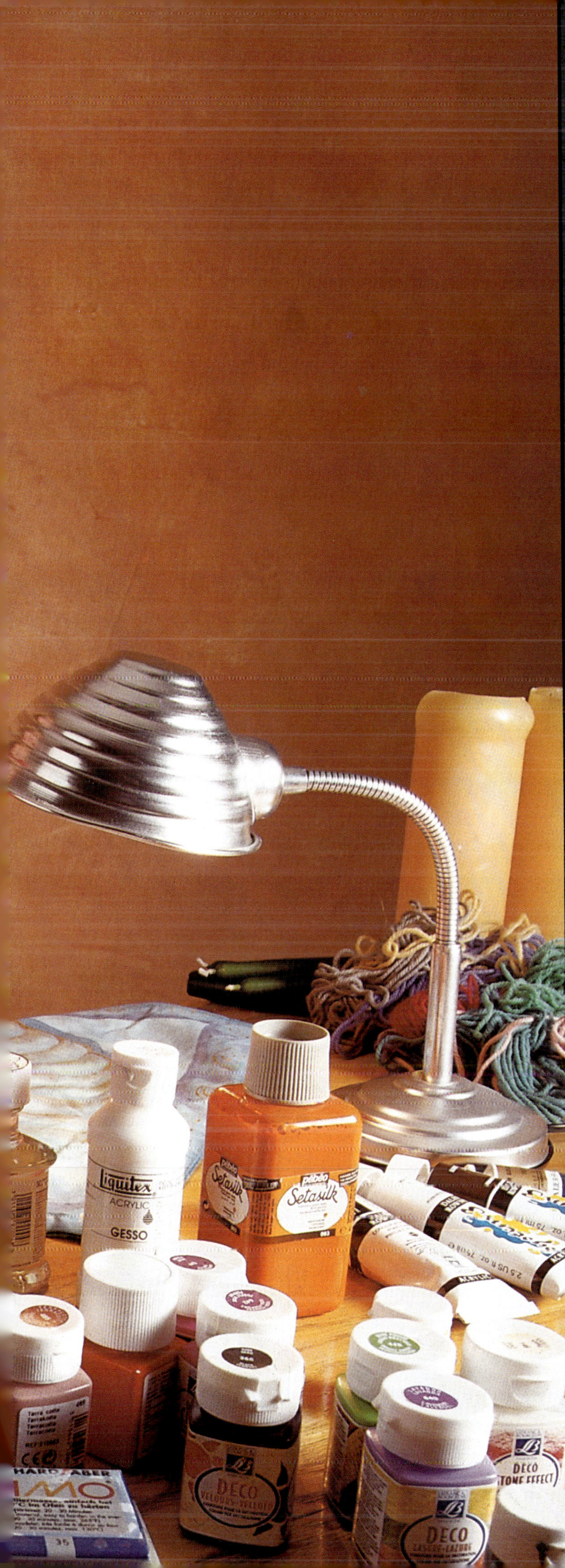

INTRODUCTION

Life today can be so hectic that spare time is all the more precious and while it would be easy to spend that spare time catching up on the domestic chores or doing extra shopping, I bet you wish you could just take a bit of time out for you occasionally and lose yourself in something absorbing and creative.

The trouble is - by the time you've got yourself organised to do anything productive it's time to stop again and you have to leave it half finished because of all the other demands on your time.

Well this book is for you - all the craft ideas in it are 'do-able' in a few hours. Believe me I've done them! If you add a call to your local craft store or artists' suppliers shop to your supermarket dash, then by the end of the day you should have created something for yourself, your home or as a gift. More importantly you will have spent a lovely creative evening which has relaxed you and certainly taken your mind off the million and one other things your children, your partner, your boss etc. want you to worry about.

Creating something in an evening with paint is easy because colour is everything.....and I offer you the options of painting on silk, glass or fabric. If you are feeling stressed out and want to 'get mellow' then go for silk painting. If you want to go a bit mad and not be tied by technique or design then sponge, stencil, stamp or freestyle paint a piece of fabric. Finally, if you are somewhere between the two and want to decorate a gift or an item for your home that will require a bit of concentration but gives impressive results....then glass painting is for you. Most importantly have fun!

Caroline Righton

PAINT

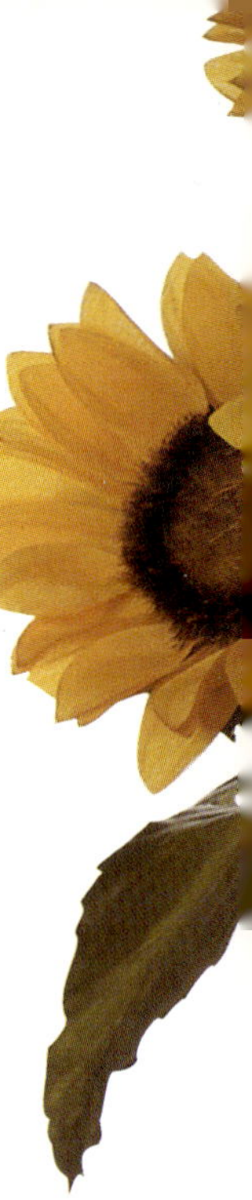

There are nine different projects in this book using paints for glass, silk or fabric....all of them easily achievable in an evening.

SILK

I have never met a single person who doesn't love the effect of charging their brush with silk colour and then just touching the material with the brush tip and watching the paint spread out to fill the space up to the line of gutta. You can silk paint very quickly and there are lots of lovely blank items available to decorate. I have done three patterns for scarves but of course you could take any elements from the patterns and trace them onto any other item, or even just turn my scarf designs into cushions or pictures.

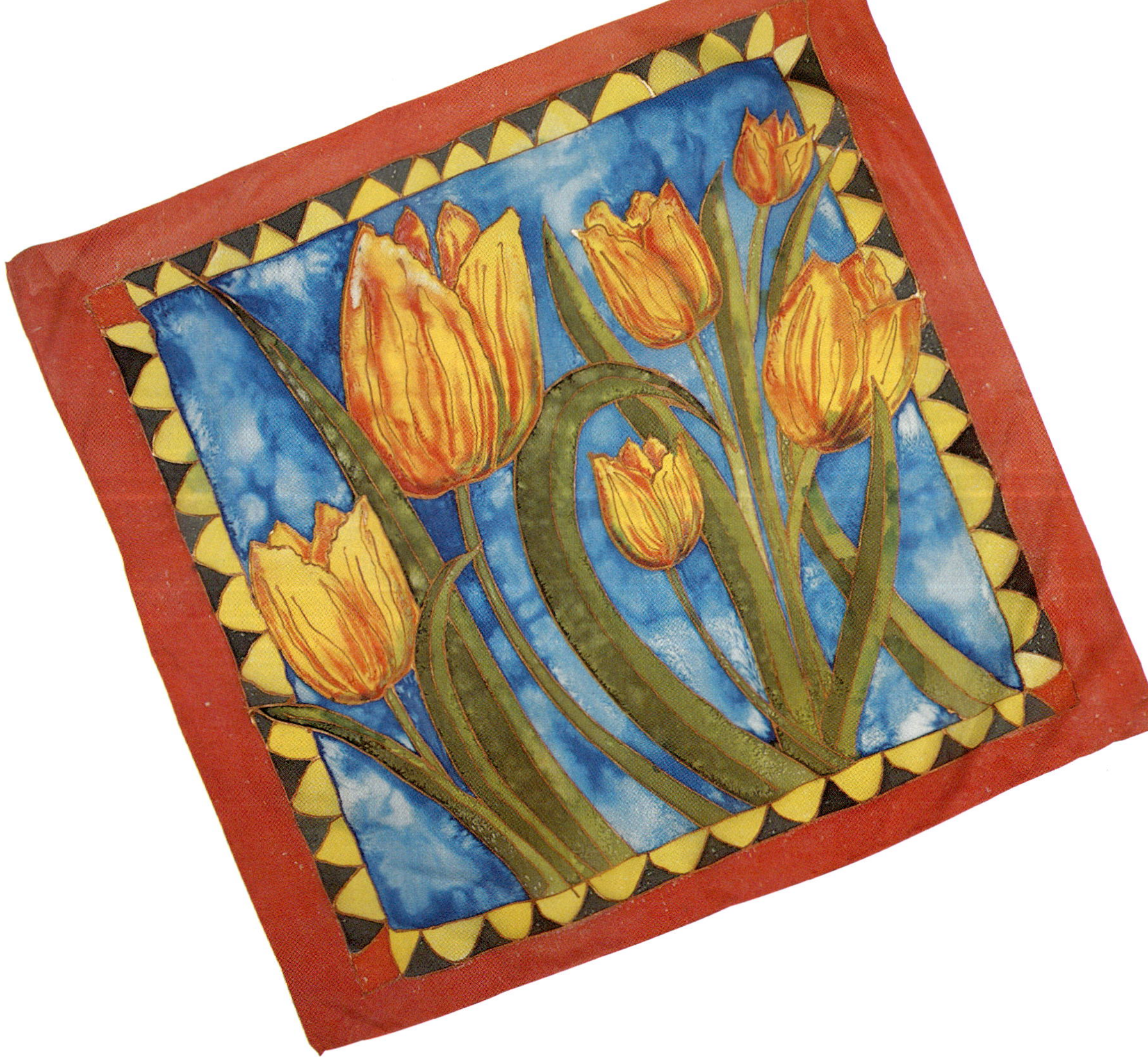

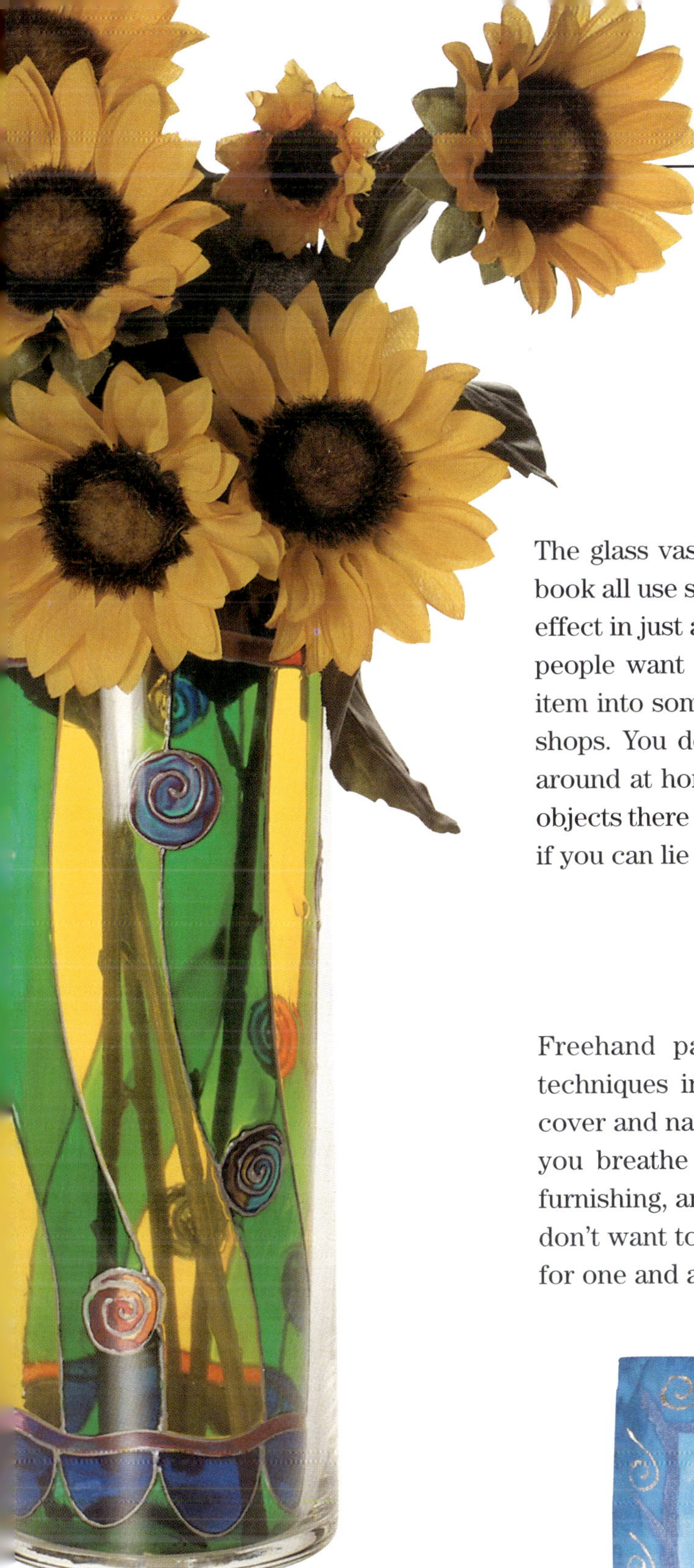

GLASS

The glass vase, boxes and suncatcher projects to glass paint in this book all use simple designs that will make it easy to achieve a striking effect in just a couple of hours. Glass painting is something that many people want to try because it really can transform a perfectly plain item into something special that would cost a great deal more in the shops. You don't need to buy the blank items I've suggested – look around at home and you'll be surprised at the number of plain glass objects there are that could be painted. From jam jars to wall mirrors... if you can lie it flat - you can paint it!

FABRIC

Freehand painting, stencilling, sponging and stamping are all techniques included on my three projects of an apron, a cushion cover and napkin set. If you don't want to buy plain items why don't you breathe new life into tired table linen or jazz up faded soft furnishing, and if you are so proud of your finished creation that you don't want to put it to practical use then adapt it into a wall-hanging for one and all to admire.

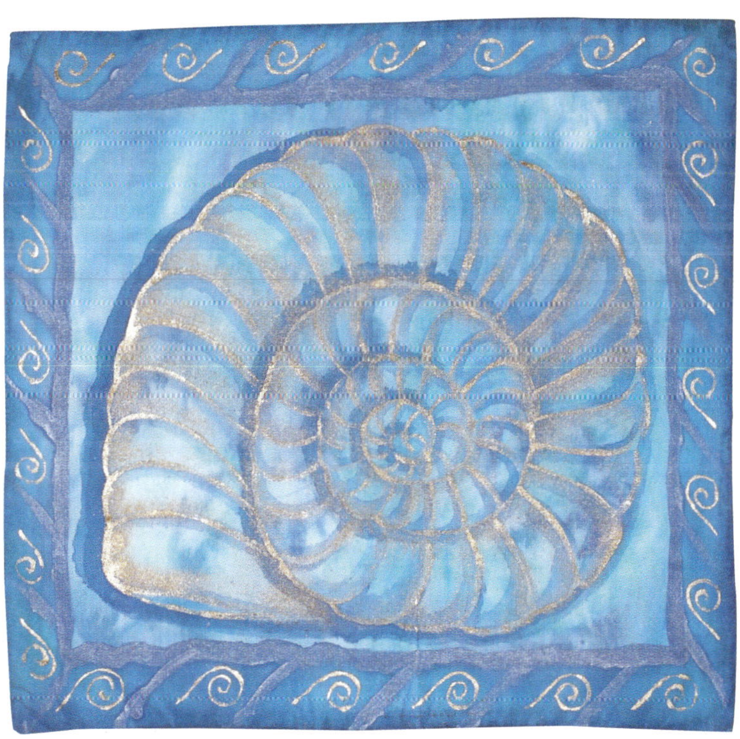

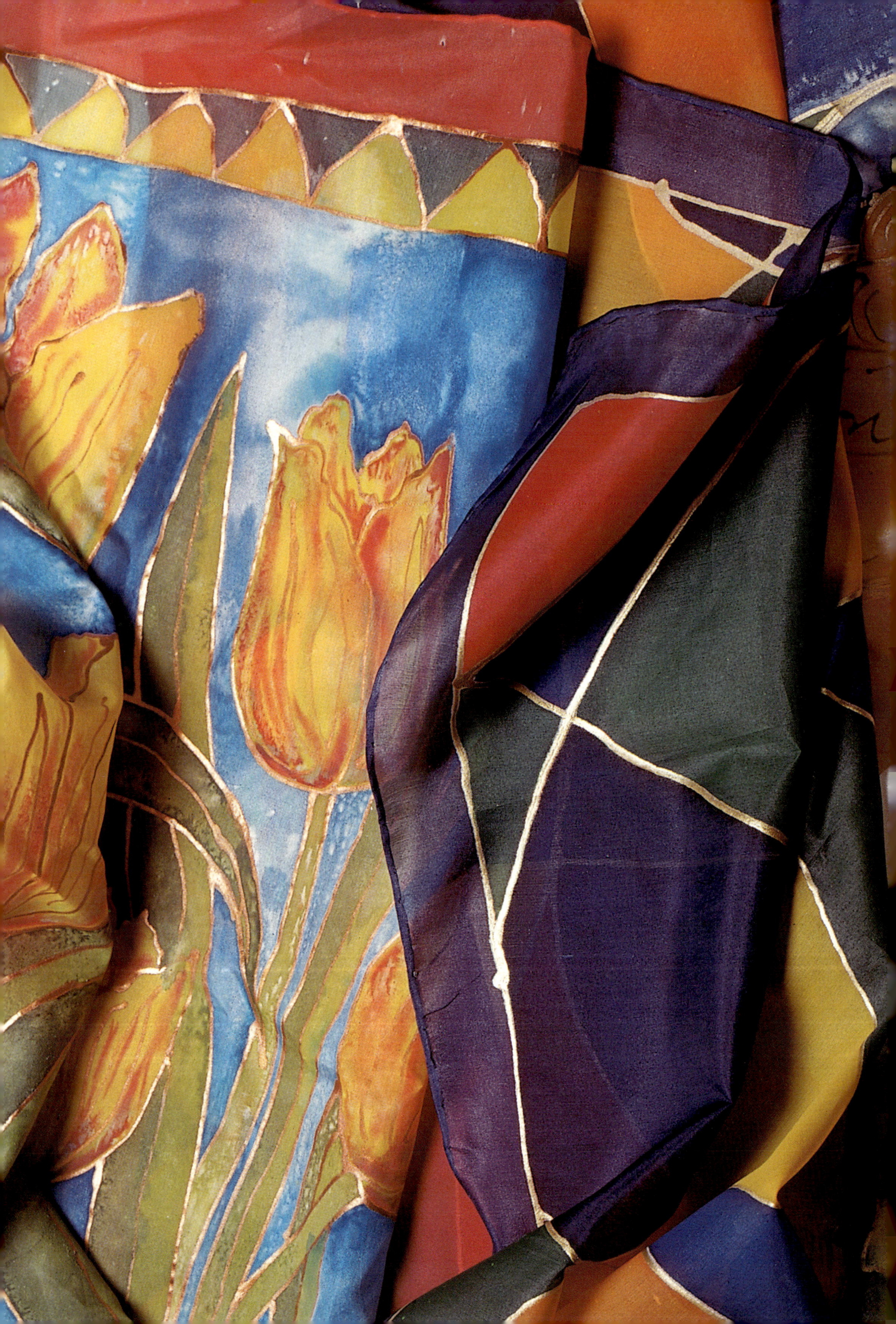

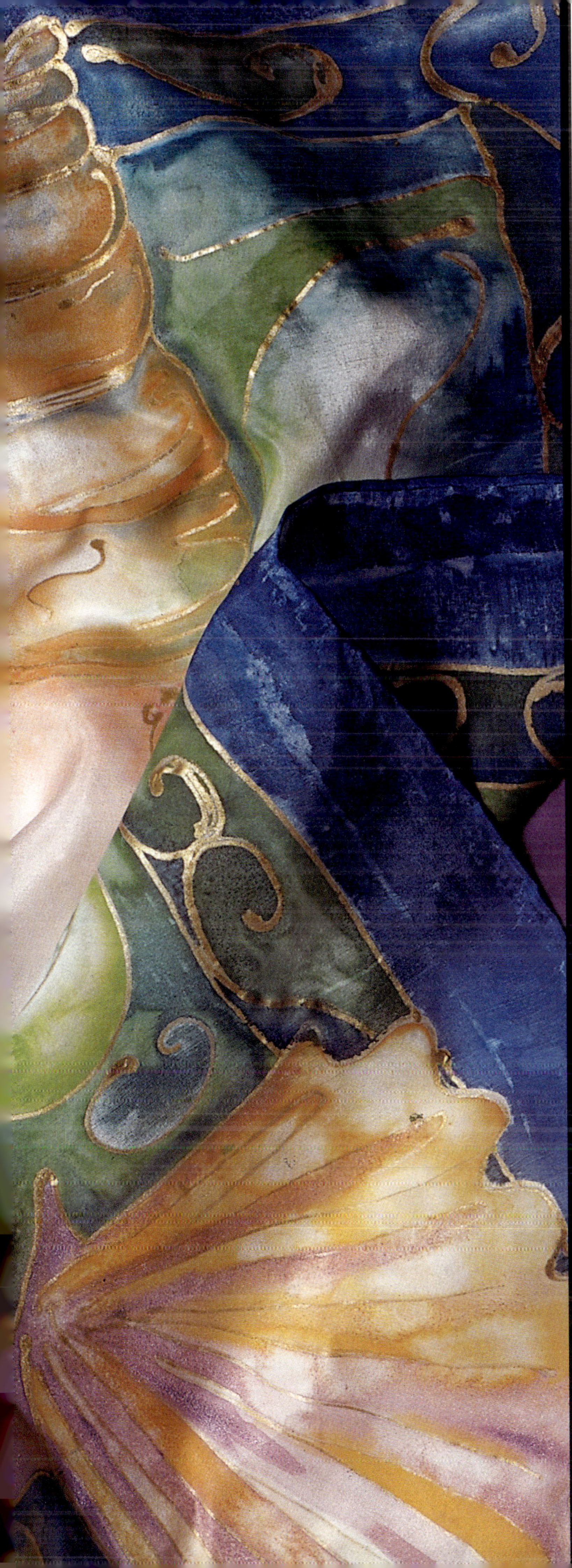

SILK
PAINTING

I hope the three silk projects I have chosen show what different effects you can achieve.

The simplest design is probably the abstract pattern but don't be put off trying the tulip or shell....they may look more complicated but they are simply more subtle and require a lighter touch! The thing to remember with silk painting is that you can always add more colour or shading so start with only a little paint and then apply more as you need to.

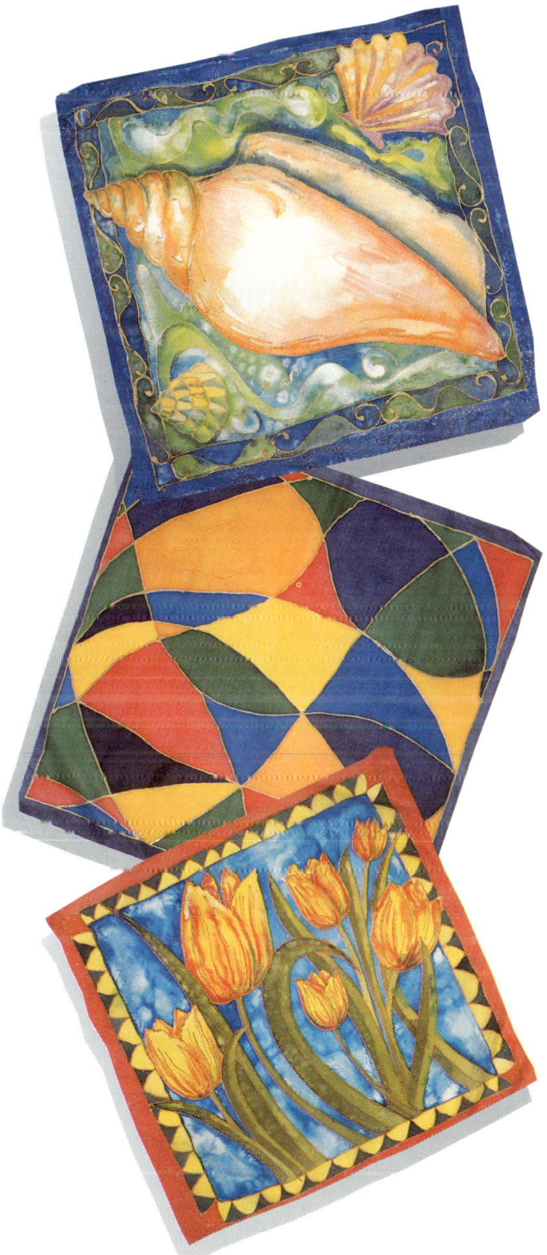

THE ORIGINS OF SILK PAINTING

It says something about the material that silk has today much of the allure that it had when it was first discovered that the 600-900 metres of silken filament that came from the cocoons produced by silkworms could be spun into the most fluid and beautiful of fabrics.

These days silk is widely available and we are all used to wearing silk clothes. But earliest records show that its use was at first confined to ornamentation and interior decoration such as wall-hangings, screens and cushions.

The first record of sericulture, as it's known, is in the 4th century BC by the Greek philosopher Aristotle on the island of Kos. We know that the Romans admired and used silk and that it was such an expensive commodity that they had to ban its import several times.

They would have been importing it from China - the natural home of silk and where silk painting is at its most beautiful and celebrated. The trade route of this fine fabric was known as the Silk Road which formed a caravan route across Central Asia through Syria and on to Rome. Alongside the silk would have been purple dye, spices, porcelain, glass and paper.

The Chinese and later the Japanese, painted birds, animals, dragons, clouds, waves, mountains and flowers upon their silk kimonos to distinguish ranks in the Imperial, noble, military and civil families.

The art of fine painting upon silk, and writing too, was highly rated among the visual arts in China. The painters used pointed-tipped brushes made of the hair of goat, deer or wolf set in a shaft of bamboo. Because the surface of silk made it so absorbent there was no room for correcting a mistake which meant these artists had to work with confidence, speed and a stunning mastery of their craft.

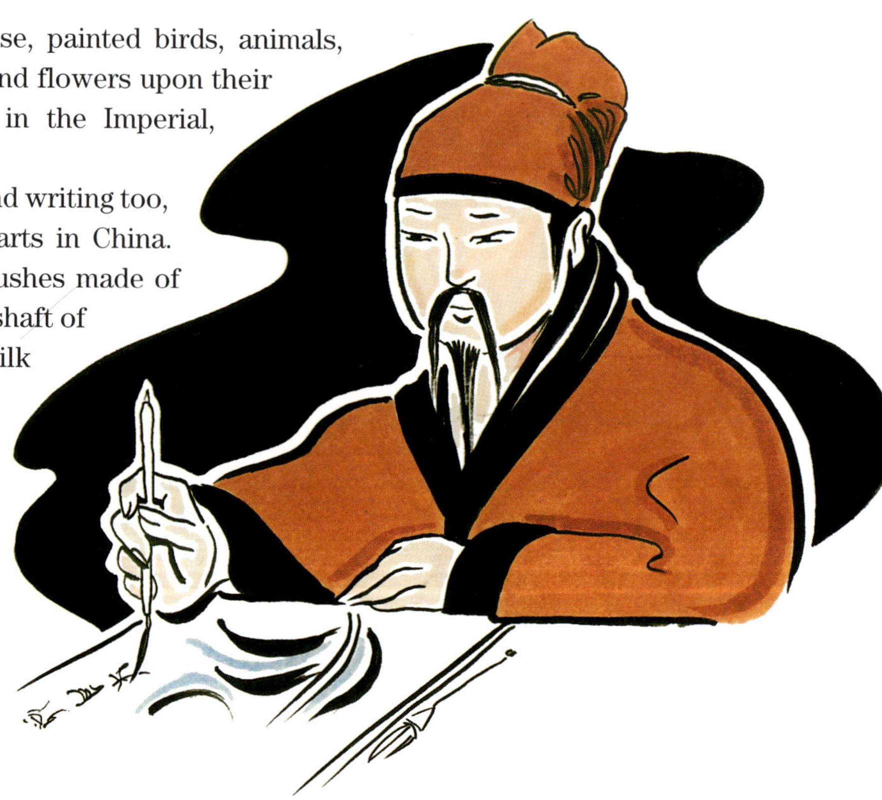

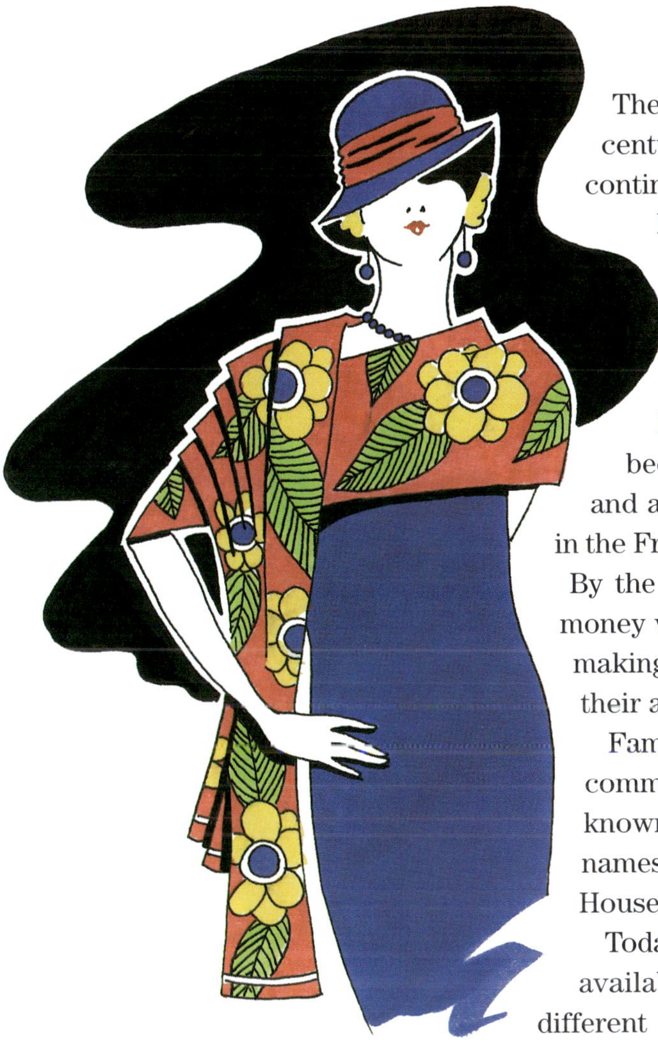

The fascination with things Oriental continued through the centuries with the bundles and rolls of silk and silk paintings continuing to be exported. Although the craft and skill of the East Asian painters was copied around the world it was always the genuine Oriental article that was most valued.

That is, until silk painting found a new interpretation in the 1920s in Europe. Many of the Russian emigres who had fled to Paris after the war found they could earn their living by decorating gentlemens' silk handkerchieves. It became fashionable to have other silk items decorated too and at one point twenty-six silk painting workshops were busy in the French capital producing wall-hangings, screens and scarves. By the end of World War Two supplies of silk were scarce and money was tight but that did not deter the fashion designers from making style statements with what was available. They turned their attention to producing decorative scarves.

Famous artists such as Henri Matisse and Henry Moore were commissioned to design silk squares, or *les carres*, as they were known. These were then reprinted in limited editions. Notable names of the time include of course Hermes and in London the House of Ascher.

Today's silk painter is unhindered by cost or availability. There are more than 20 different grades of silk fabric that can be bought, some very cheaply.

It's available by the metre in a range of textures and weights. There are plain fashion items and silk products for the home including plain white silk flowers and window decorations.

It may be a long way from the imperial wall-hangings of the Ming dynasty in China all those centuries ago – but silk painting is now accessible to all.

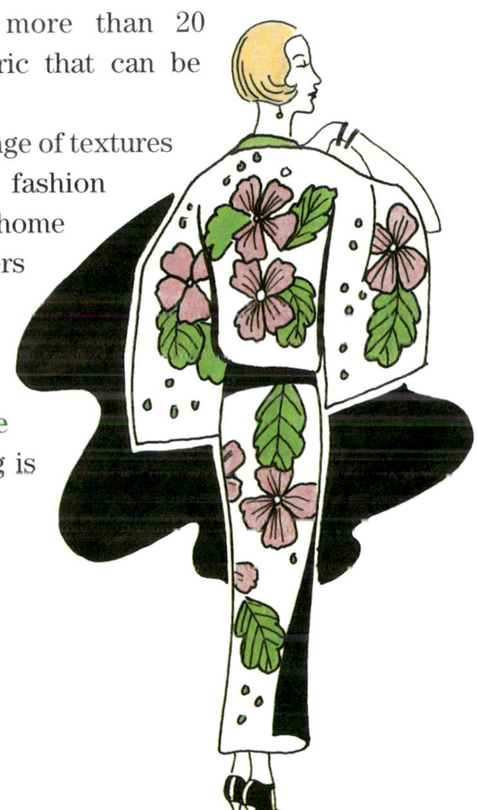

Gutta

Paint

Frame

Silk

Pattern

Kitchen roll

Salt

Pins

Pencil

Brushes

Water

Palette

Iron

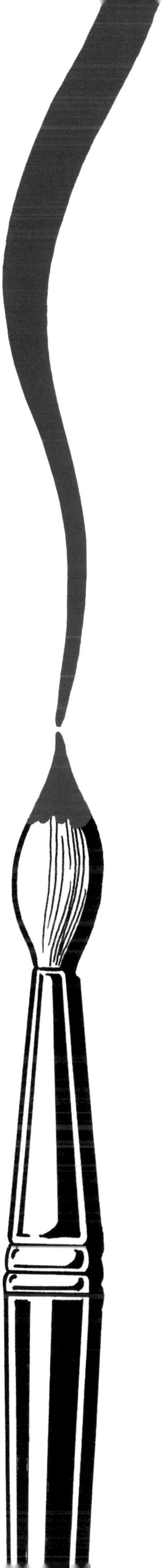

EQUIPMENT

The equipment you need to silk paint is very straightforward... and is basically the same as would have been used by the ancient Chinese.

Silk: these days you can buy ready-made blank items such as scarves, ties, hats etc, or pre-cut lengths (90 x 100 cm) or you can buy it by the metre. It is classified by its weight per square metre. The usual unit of measurement is 'momme'. This is equal to a silk weight of 4.306 grams per square metre. For example ponge 5 means the silk grade is 5 momme which is approximately 33 grams per square metre. The most common types of silk used for those taking up silk painting as a craft are ponge, habotai, crépe de chine and crépe satin.

Gutta: is a form of gum or resin which is used to draw a pattern on the silk. The lines of gutta stop the silk paint colours from spreading into each other. Gutta is available in lots of different colours and also transparent.

Paints: there are many different makes on the market including colours in pen form.

Brushes: you can use any soft pointed brush. If you discover you love the craft then treat yourself to one of the bound bamboo brushes.

Frame: the frame serves to lift the silk away from the surface and keep it taut. There are several types on the market, adjustable wooden ones and plastic self-gripping frames. Or you can construct your own from pieces of wood or rigid polystyrene.

Pins: you'll need pins to hold your silk tautly in place on the frame - and you can buy special silk pins which don't leave marks.

Palette: you will get the best effects by diluting and mixing colours so you'll need either a specially bought divided paint palette or several old saucers.

Pencil: for lightly tracing out your design on the silk before applying the gutta if you want to - I don't bother personally.

Salt: to achieve a special effect, see techniques.

Kitchen roll: useful for mopping up and blotting.

Water: for diluting the paint and cleaning your brush between colours.

Pattern: the design you plan to follow.

Iron and clean white cloth: for 'fixing' the paints so the item can be gently washed.

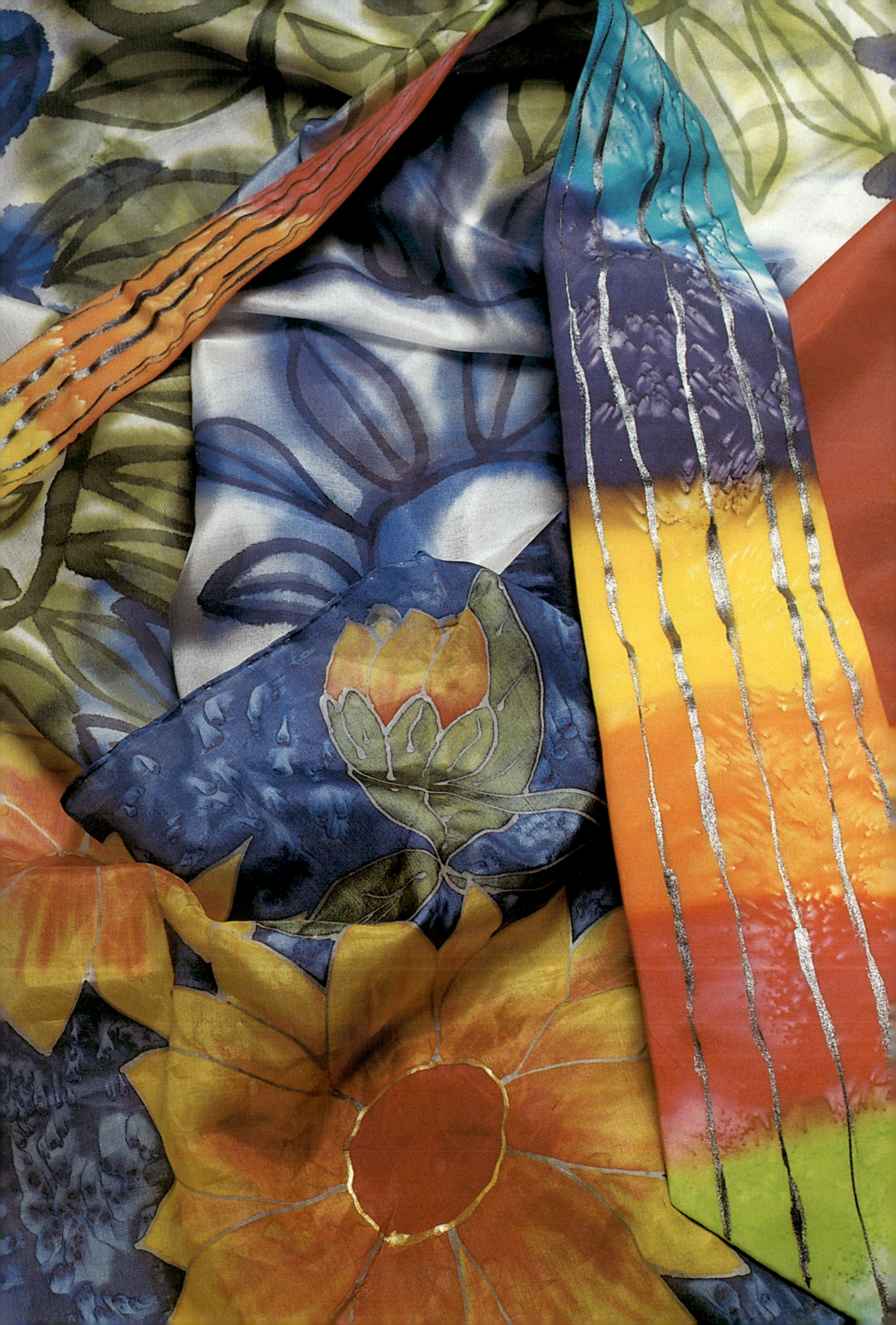

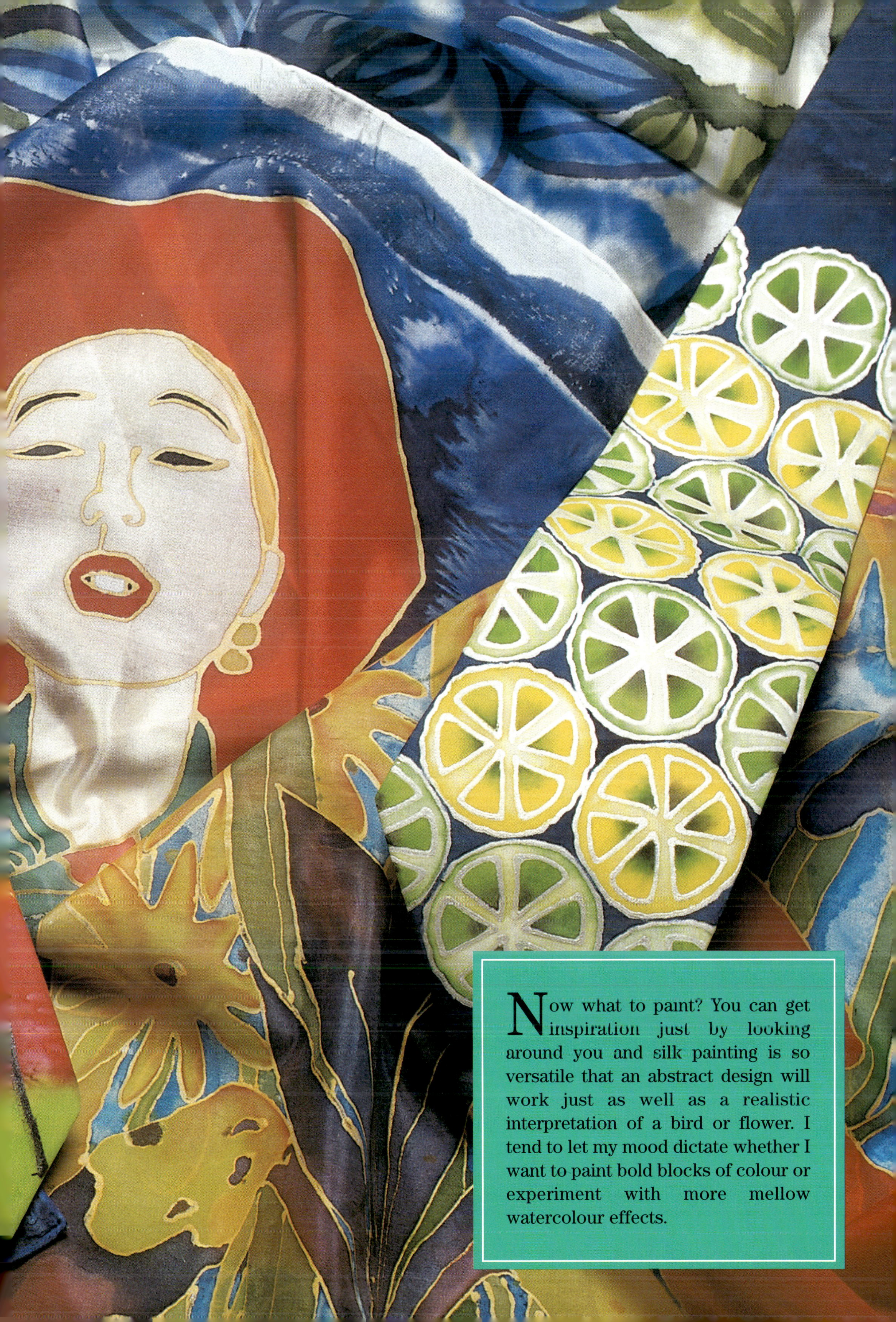

Now what to paint? You can get inspiration just by looking around you and silk painting is so versatile that an abstract design will work just as well as a realistic interpretation of a bird or flower. I tend to let my mood dictate whether I want to paint bold blocks of colour or experiment with more mellow watercolour effects.

TECHNIQUES

There are many different and beautiful effects you can achieve when you paint on silk. It is a very forgiving medium and I've often found that some of my most stunning creations have started out as mistakes!

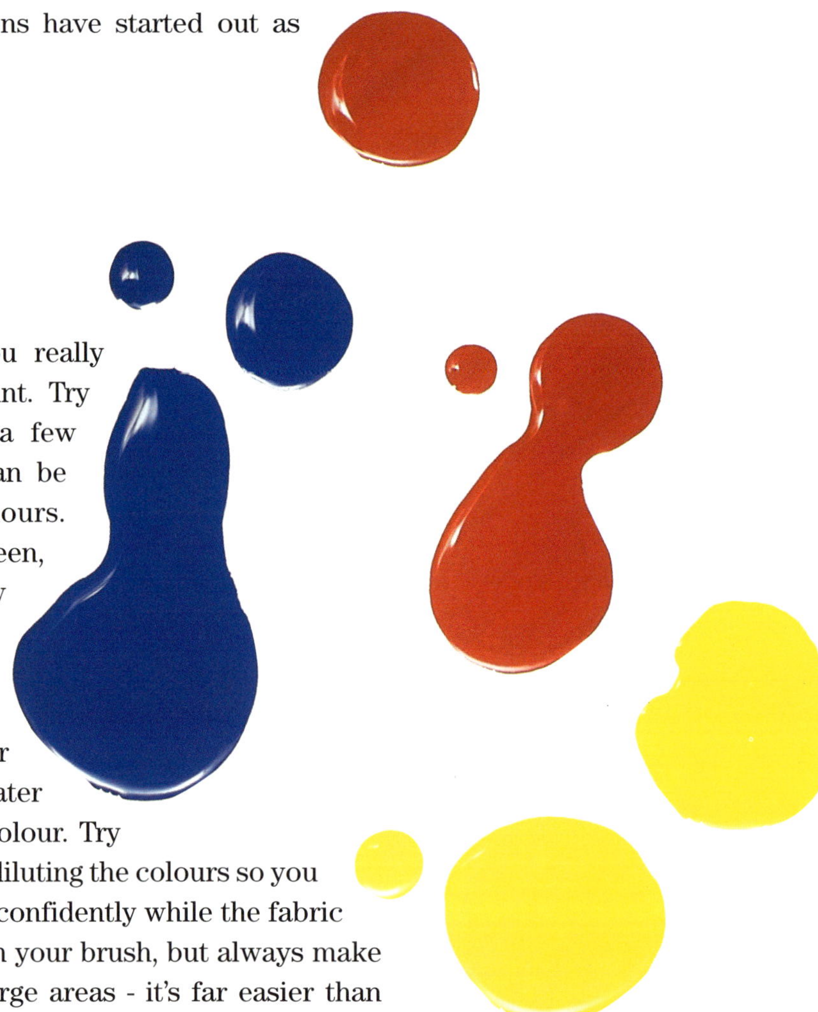

COLOUR

I can't recommend too highly that you really experiment with colour before you paint. Try mixing them - even if you only buy a few primary colours to start with - they can be mixed to make lots of different colours. Remember blue and yellow will make green, blue and red will make purple and yellow and red will make orange. Use tiny amounts to mix with initially - literally just dip the tip of your brush into the paint pot then dab it onto your palette or saucer before washing the brush in the water and then dipping it again into another colour. Try layering one colour over another and try diluting the colours so you achieve a wash effect. Work quickly and confidently while the fabric is still damp. You need very little paint on your brush, but always make sure you mix enough colour to fill in large areas - it's far easier than trying to make an exact match later on. Always start painting with the lighter colours and keep your kitchen towel or a clean cloth handy - you can blot excess paint.

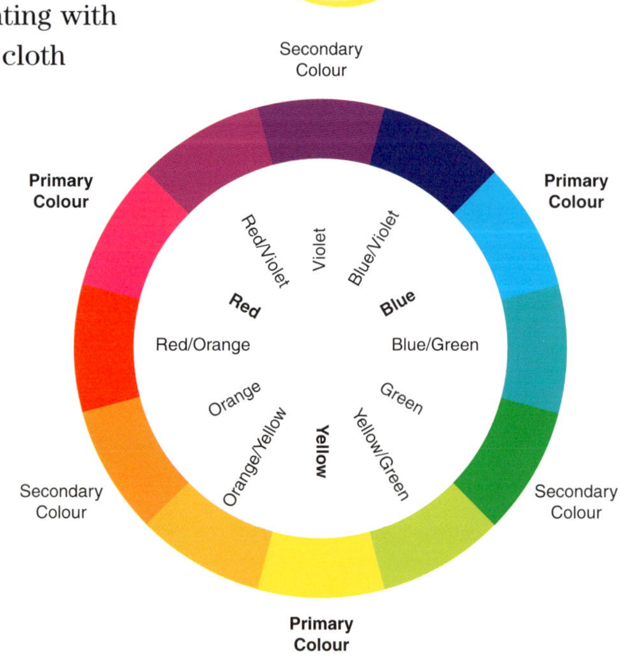

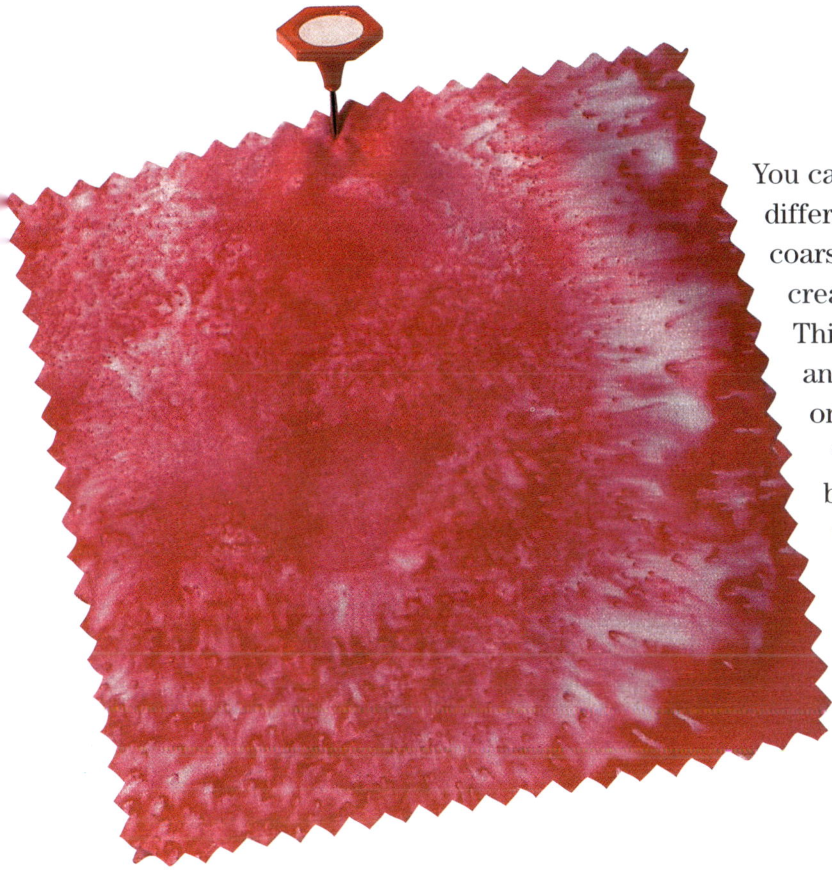

SALT

You can achieve special effects by using a couple of different techniques. For example, if you sprinkle coarse sea salt onto newly painted wet silk you will create wonderful swirls and patterns of colour. This is caused by the salt absorbing the moisture and paint. Carefully brush and shake the salt off once the silk is completely dry. This technique works well wherever you want to break up blocks of colour and give an impression of texture. It is also a good way to stop a background being too dominant yet adding interest at the same time.

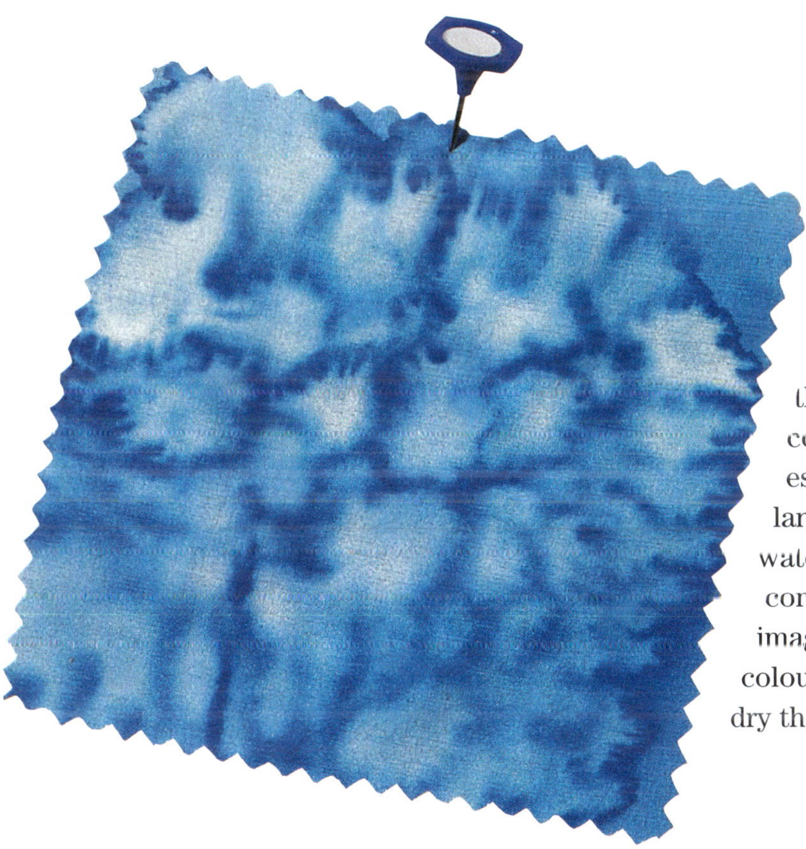

WATER

Another technique involves experimenting with using different amounts of water mixed with your colour.

Paint one colour as a wash background and then while the fabric is still wet use another colour to draw your shapes and figures. This is especially effective if you want to draw landscapes or pictures in a similar way to using watercolour paints on paper. Also when the silk is completely dry you can draw stronger lines and images using the wet on dry technique. If the colours start running or 'bleeding' too much then dry the area with a hair dryer whilst painting.

STEP-BY-STEP

The first thing to do is to iron out all the creases in your silk and to assemble all the paints, brushes, palettes, and other items you intend to use. Because you will need to work quickly once you start it's important to get yourself organised at the beginning and that includes making the cup of tea etc.

THE FRAME

Construct your frame as instructed or if you have bought wood or polystyrene to make your own, cut lengths slightly longer than your silk, cut the ends diagonally and nail or pin as in the diagram ensuring each corner is securely fixed. This is important because your silk must be stretched onto a frame to prevent contact with the surface below.

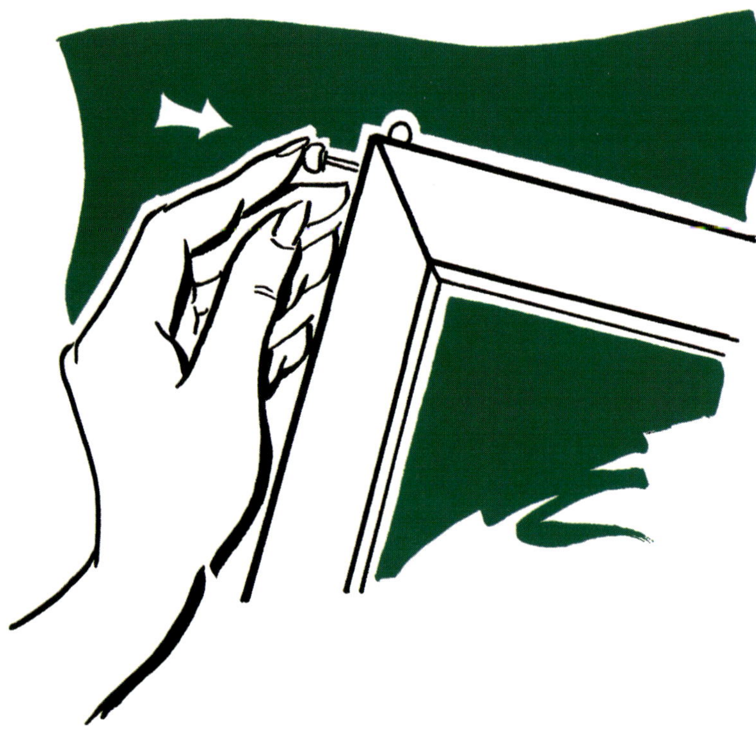

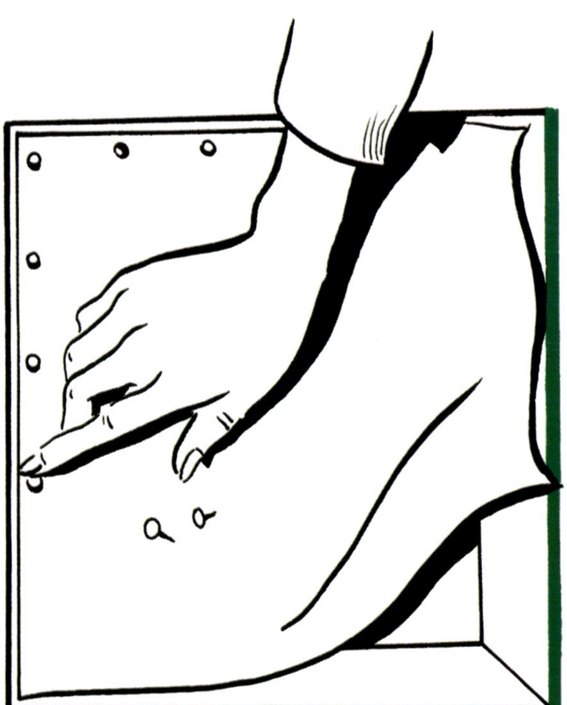

Pin your silk tautly onto the frame as shown in the diagram.

GUTTA

Unless you are going to paint freehand, place a piece of paper with your chosen design on underneath the frame and silk and, holding the tube of gutta like a pen, squeeze it out in a thin line onto the silk tracing over the design. Work as quickly and as smoothly as you can. Leave to dry for approximately 30 minutes.

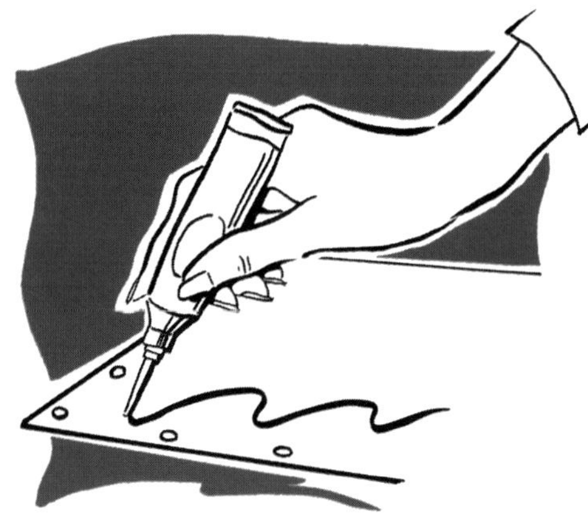

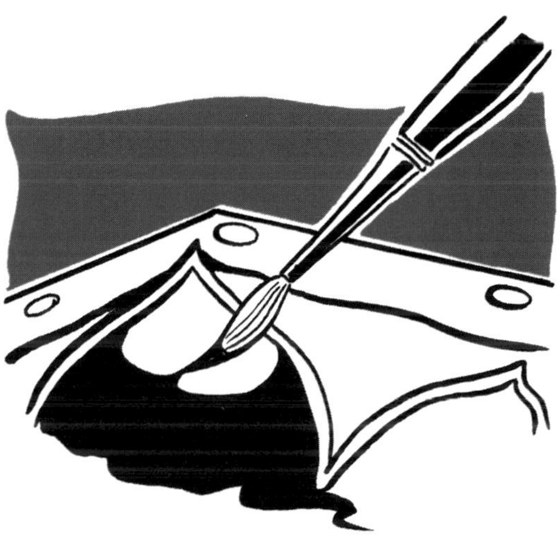

PAINTING

Now you are ready to start painting. Shake the bottles well before opening. Always start painting in the middle of a space and let the paint spread by itself to the gutta outline. Leaving the border until the very end, start painting in the top left-hand corner (if you are right-handed). When you paint the border carefully lift the pins individually and replace them lightly as you paint making sure you don't press them too hard into the painted silk.

FIXING

Remove the scarf from the frame when it is completely dry. Place it face down on an ironing board and cover with a clean cotton cloth before ironing continuously for about seven minutes with the iron on cotton setting. Some paints require different fixing methods so check the manufacturer's instructions.

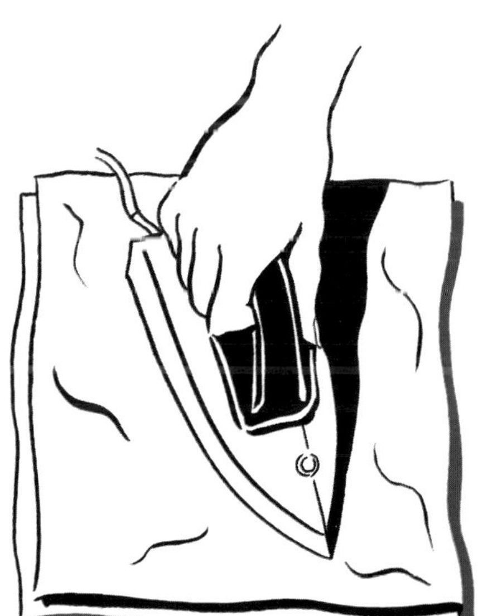

PATTERN

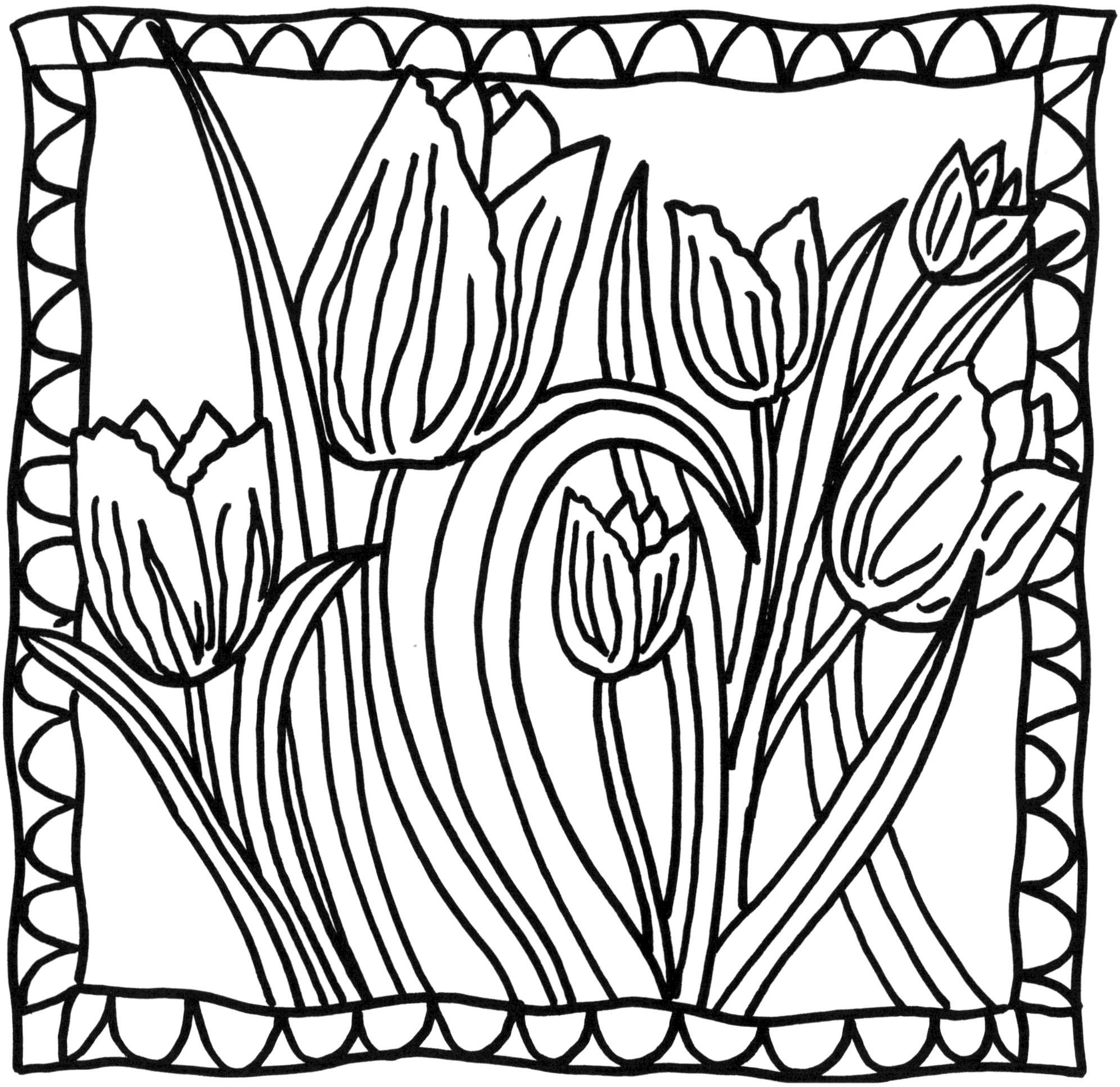

YOU WILL NEED

- A copy of this pattern photocopied and enlarged to the size of your silk
- Silk - I've used a pre-hemmed silk square 55cm x 55cm
- Red, yellow and blue silk paints
- Bronze gutta
- A brush
- A frame
- Silk pins
- An iron

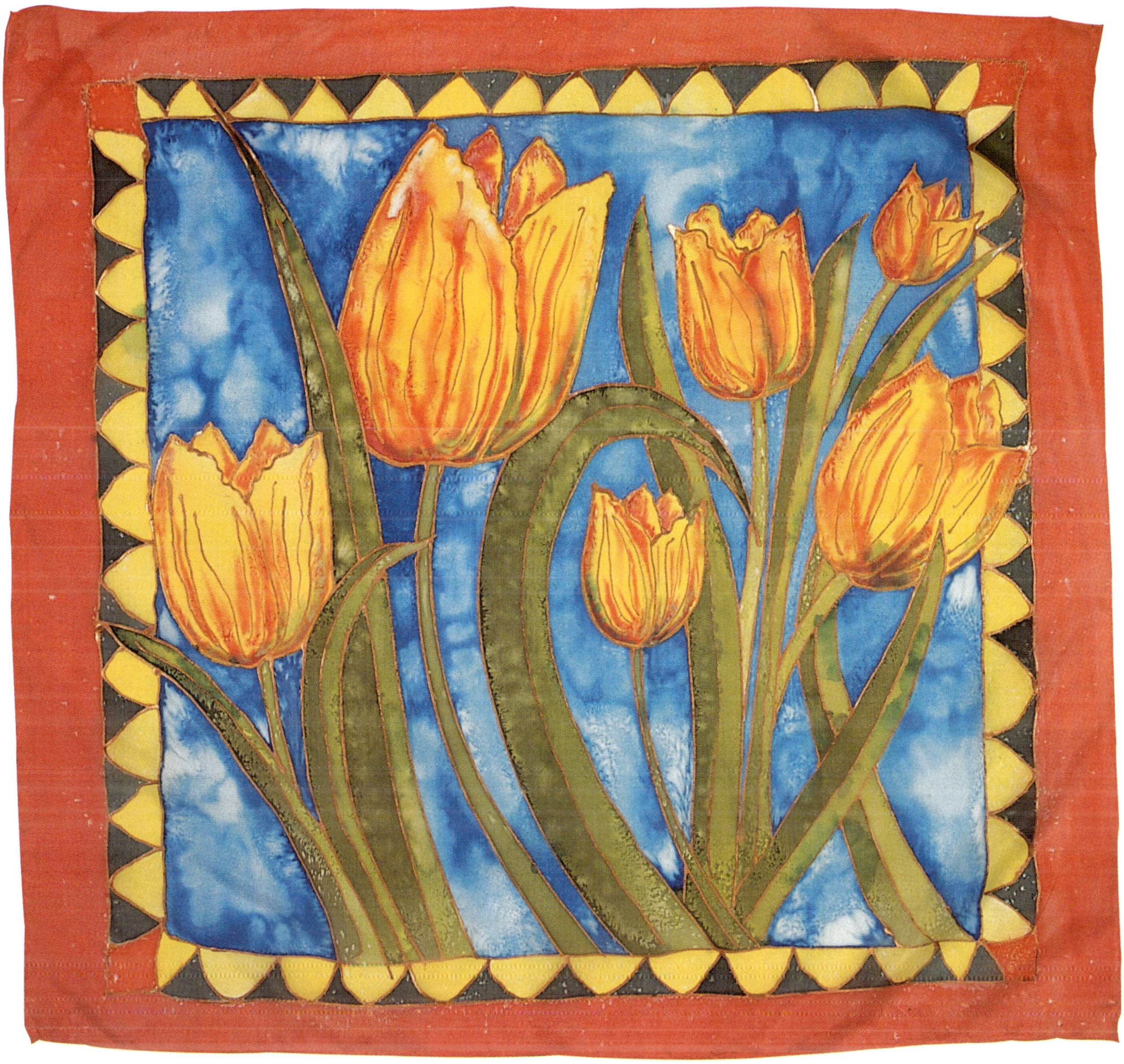

The Japanese immortalised chrysanthemums on their silk paintings and I really think flowers lend themselves particularly well to this medium. I love tulips and hope you like the vibrant shades of these blooms. It will give you a chance to practise mixing basic colours - although, of course, tulips come in all shades - perhaps yours will be purple!

PATTERN

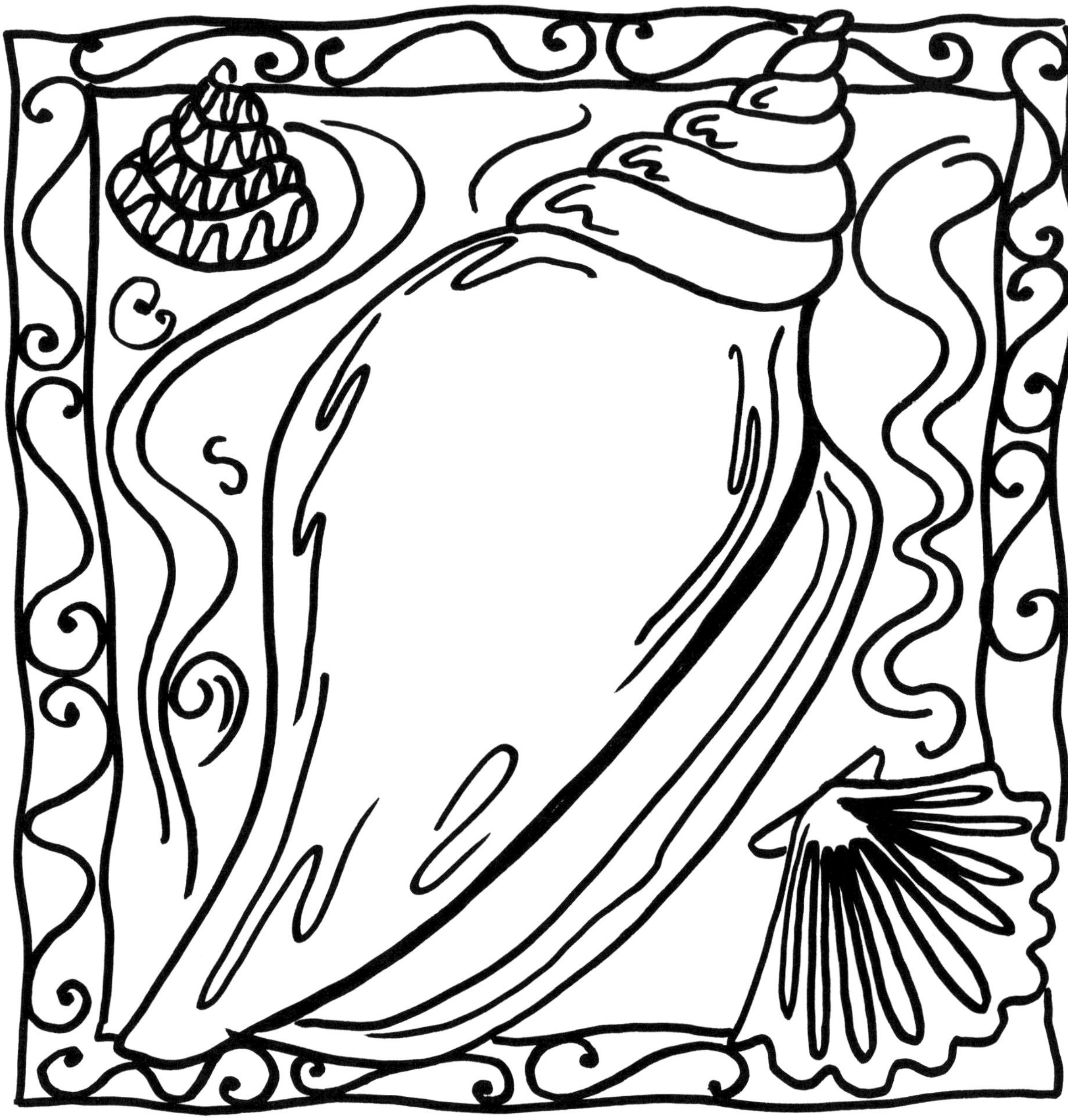

YOU WILL NEED

A copy of this pattern photocopied and enlarged to the size of your silk

- Silk - I've used a pre-hemmed silk square 55cm x 55cm
- Red, yellow and blue silk paints
- Gold or silver gutta
- A brush
- A frame
- Silk pins
- An iron

SHELL SCARF

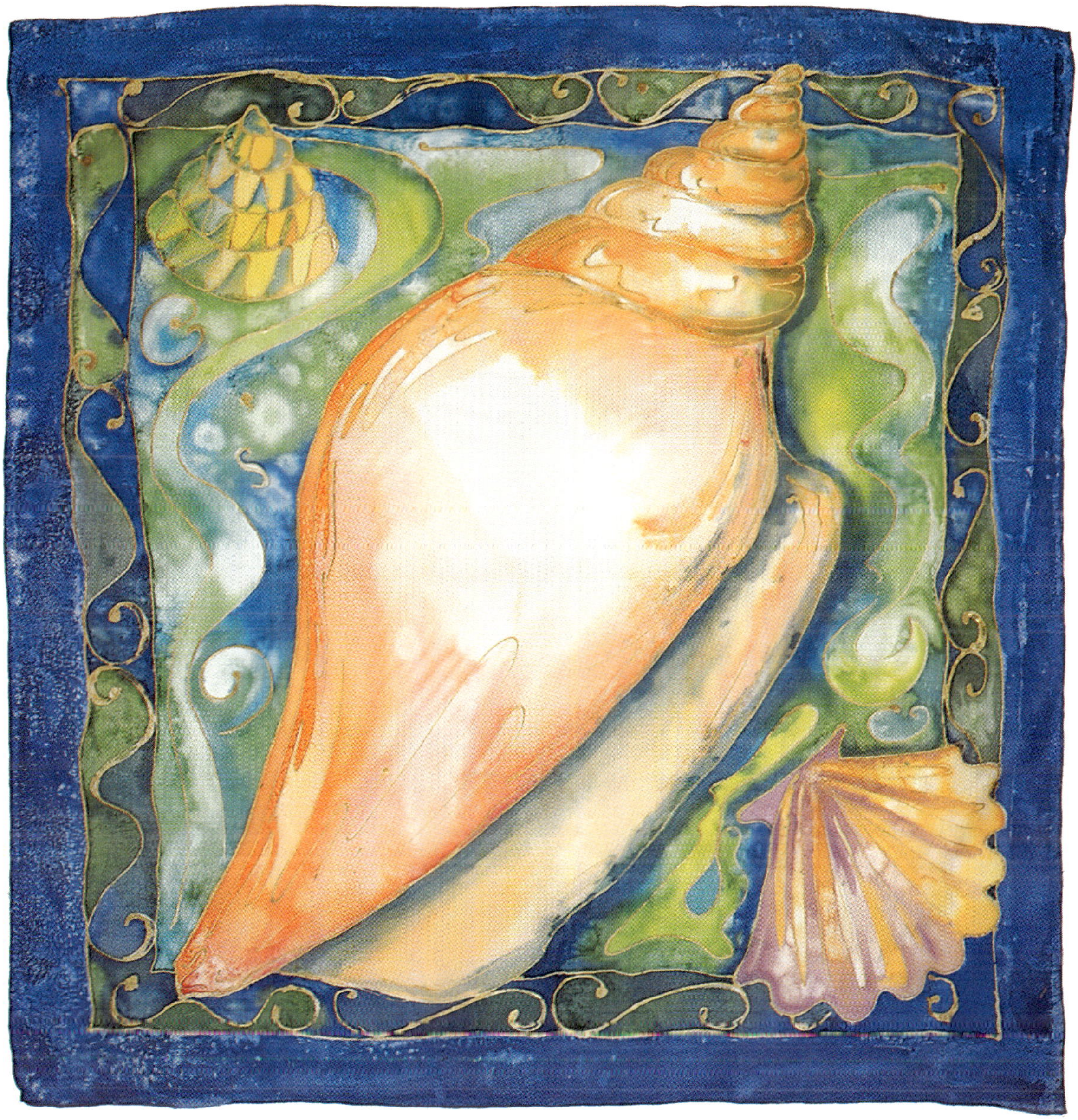

Something less rather than more is what's called for if you want to achieve the iridescent effect on this shell design by using very little paint in the centre and letting the natural sheen of the fabric catch the light in the same way as real pearly shell.

PATTERN

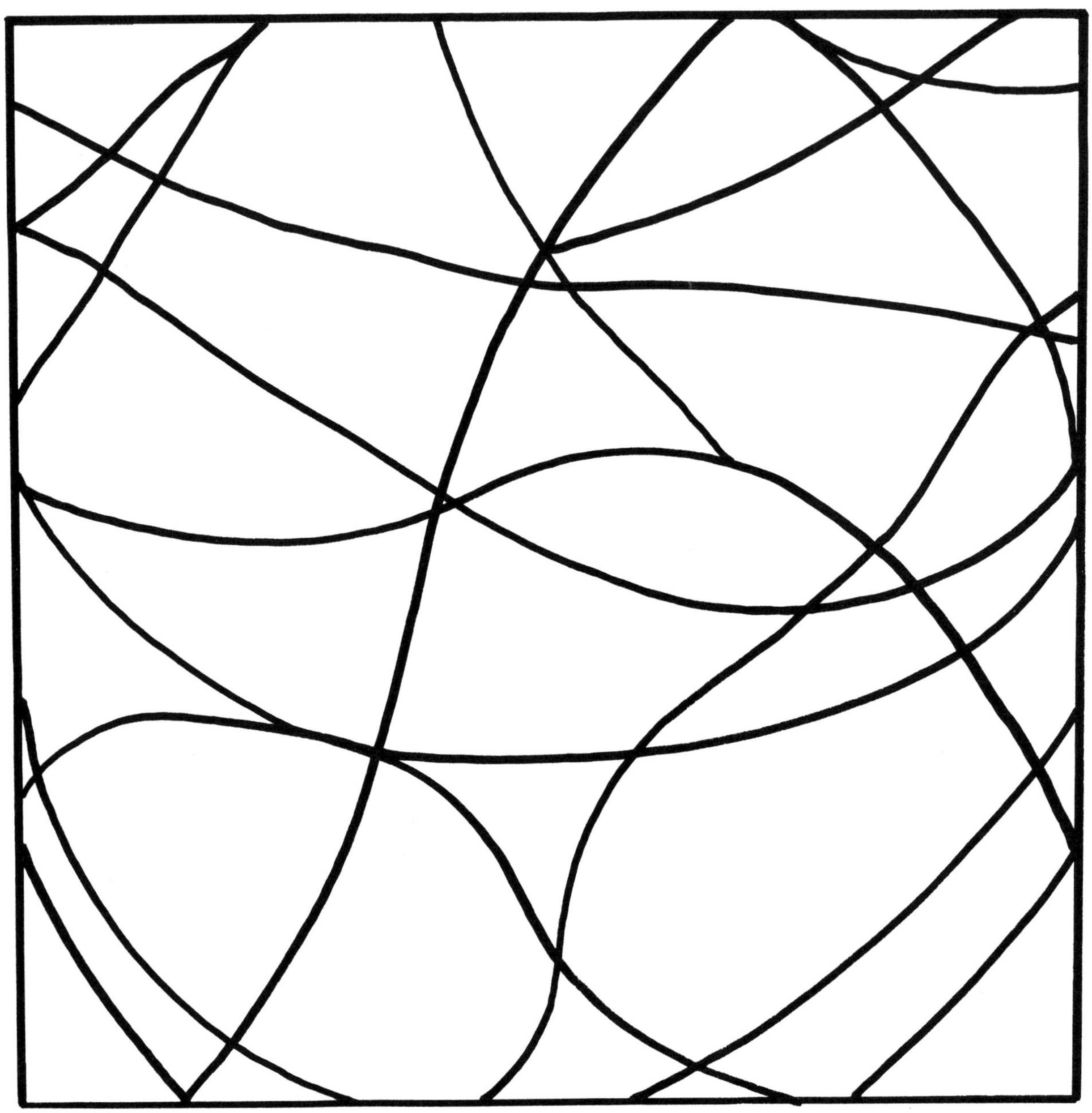

YOU WILL NEED

- A copy of this pattern photocopied and enlarged to the size of your silk
- Silk - I've used a pre-hemmed silk square 55cm x 55cm
- Red yellow and blue silk paints
- Gold gutta
- A brush
- A frame
- Silk pins
- An iron

ABSTRACT SCARF

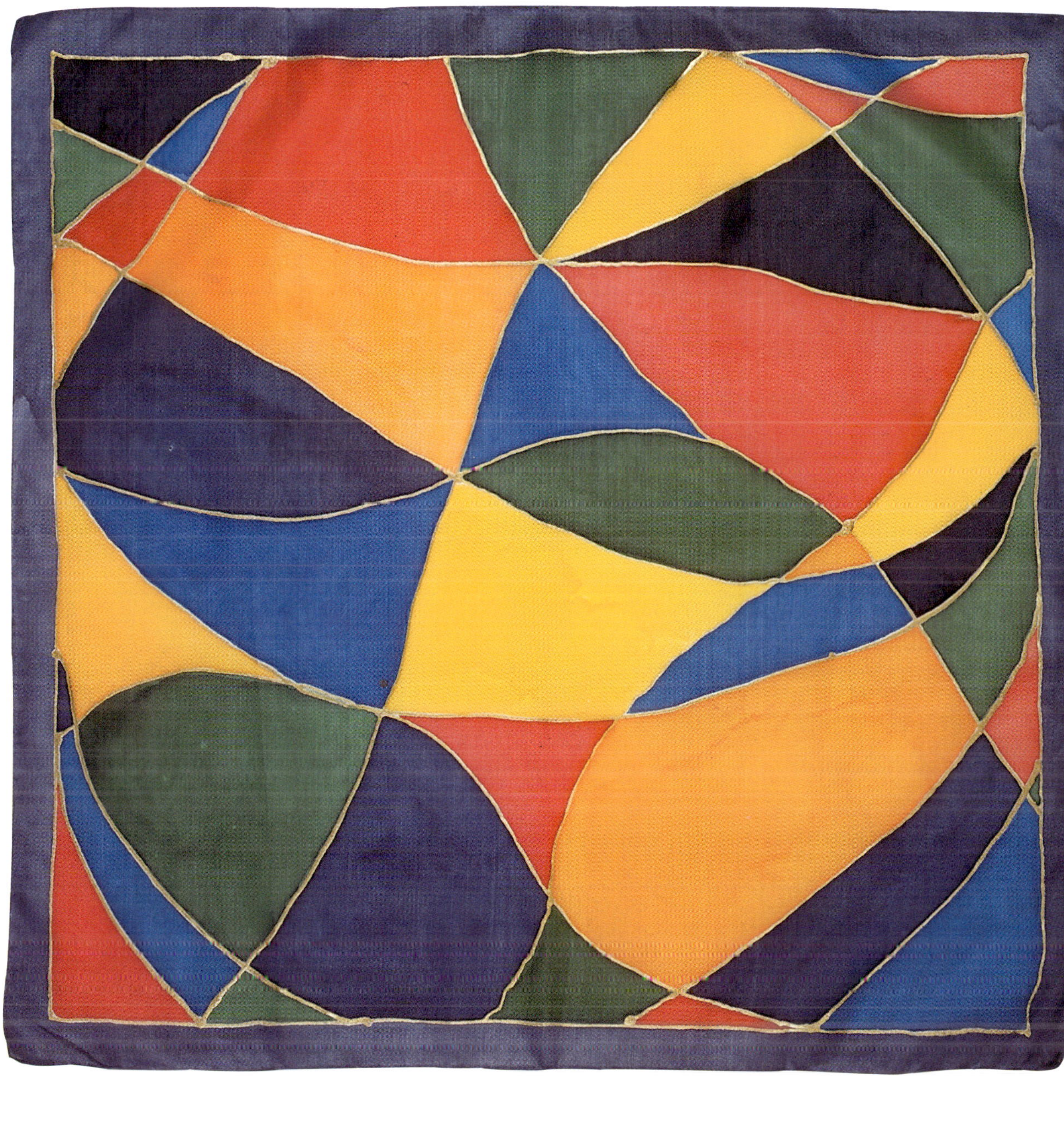

Take as a theme this abstract design and have fun with colour. It will be hard to go wrong and you are virtually guaranteed a stunning result.

WHY STOP AT SCARVES

when there are so many other gorgeous things made from silk just waiting for you to decorate?

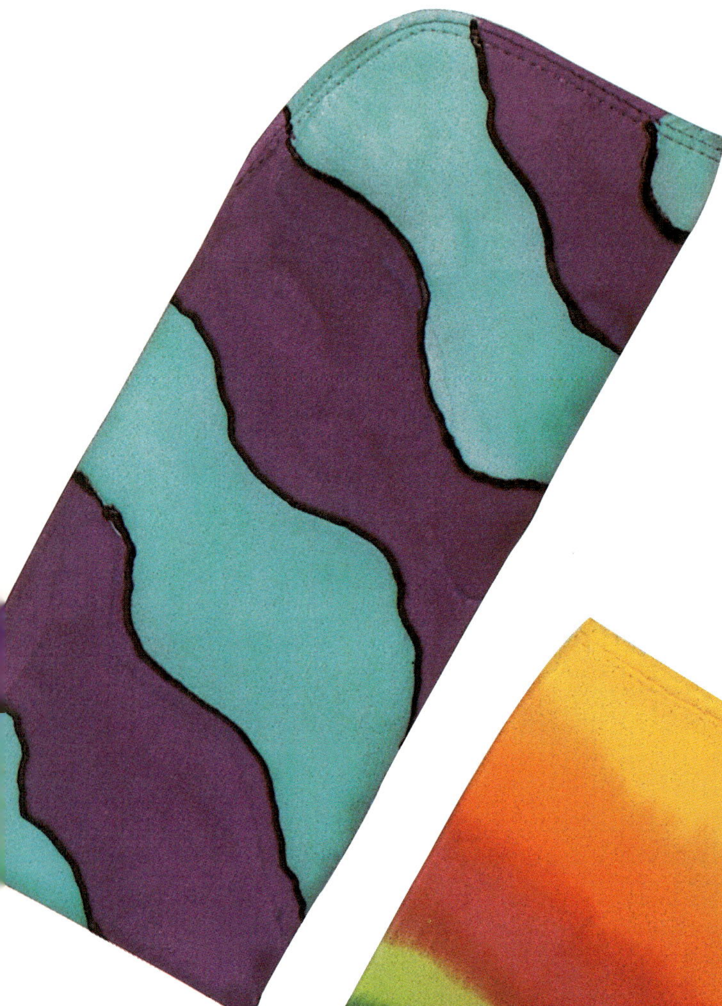

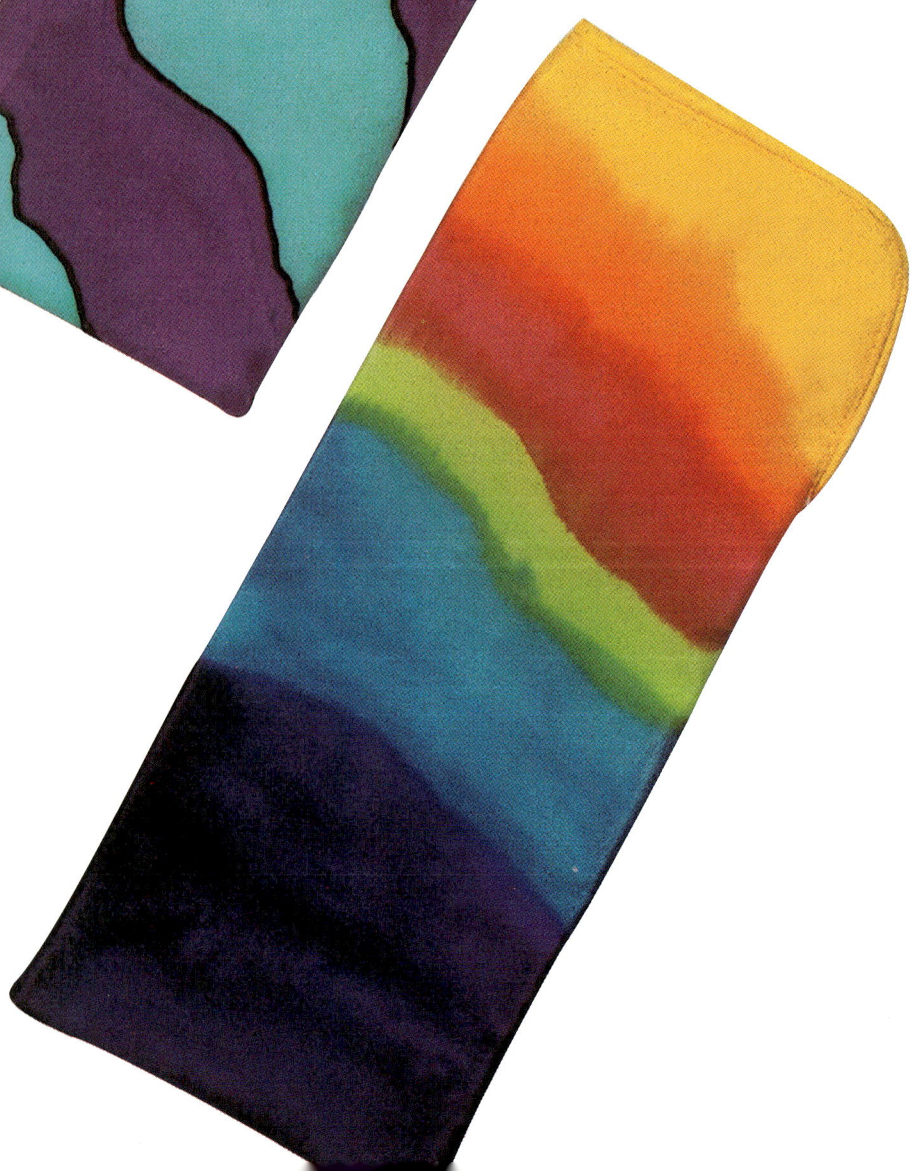

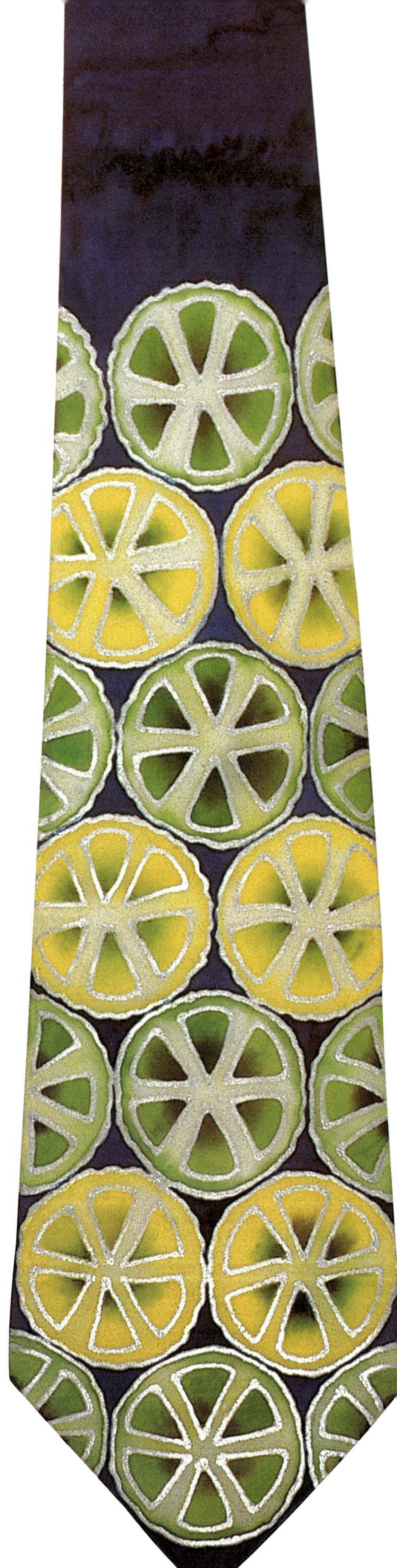

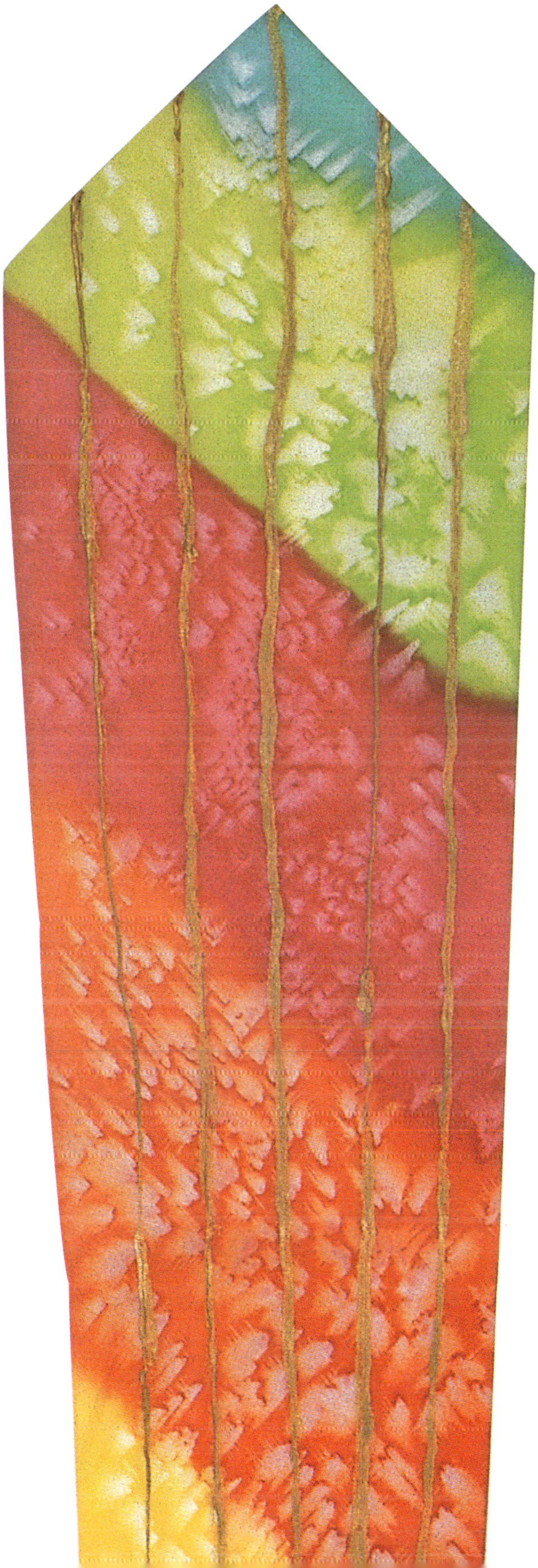

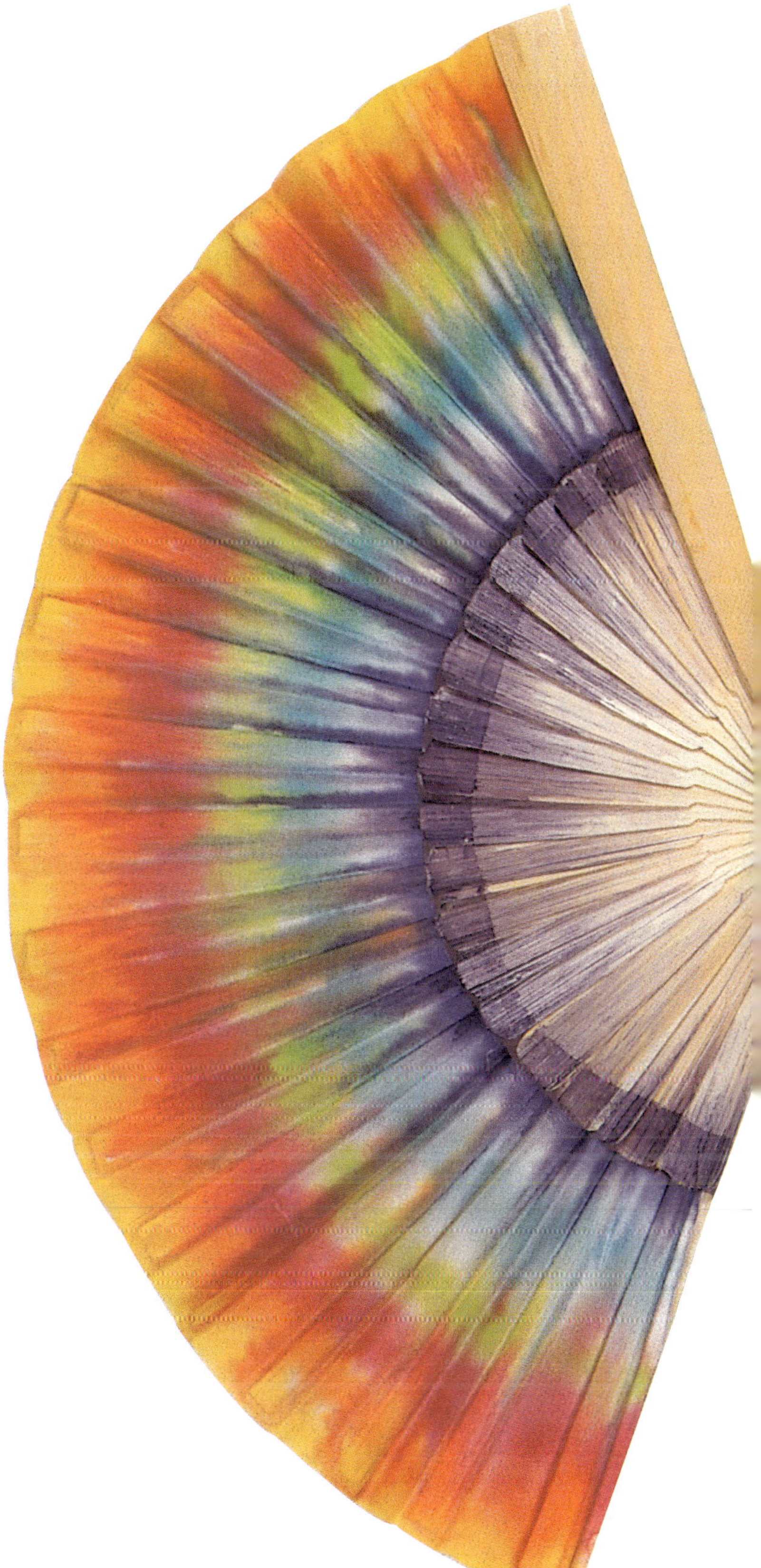

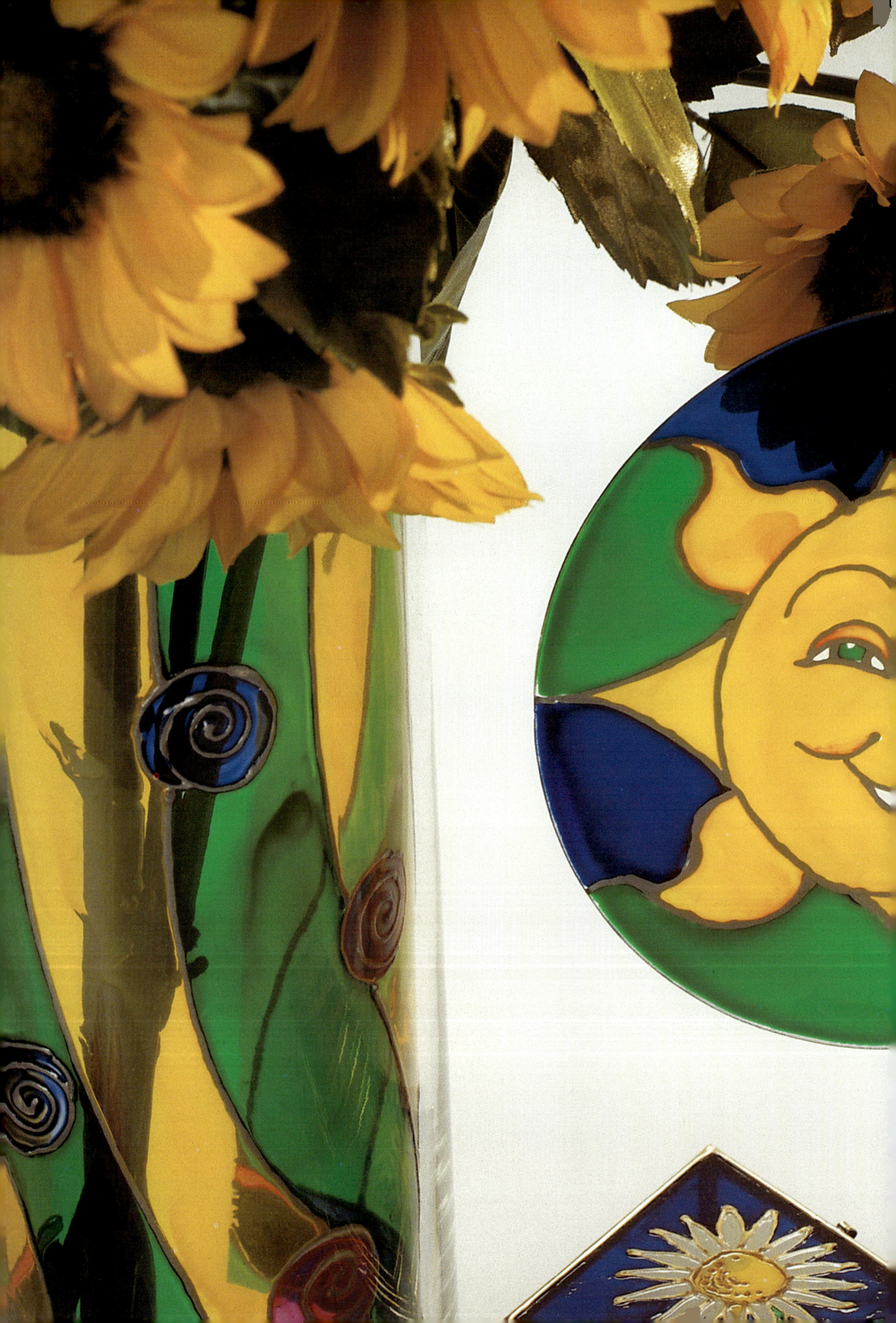

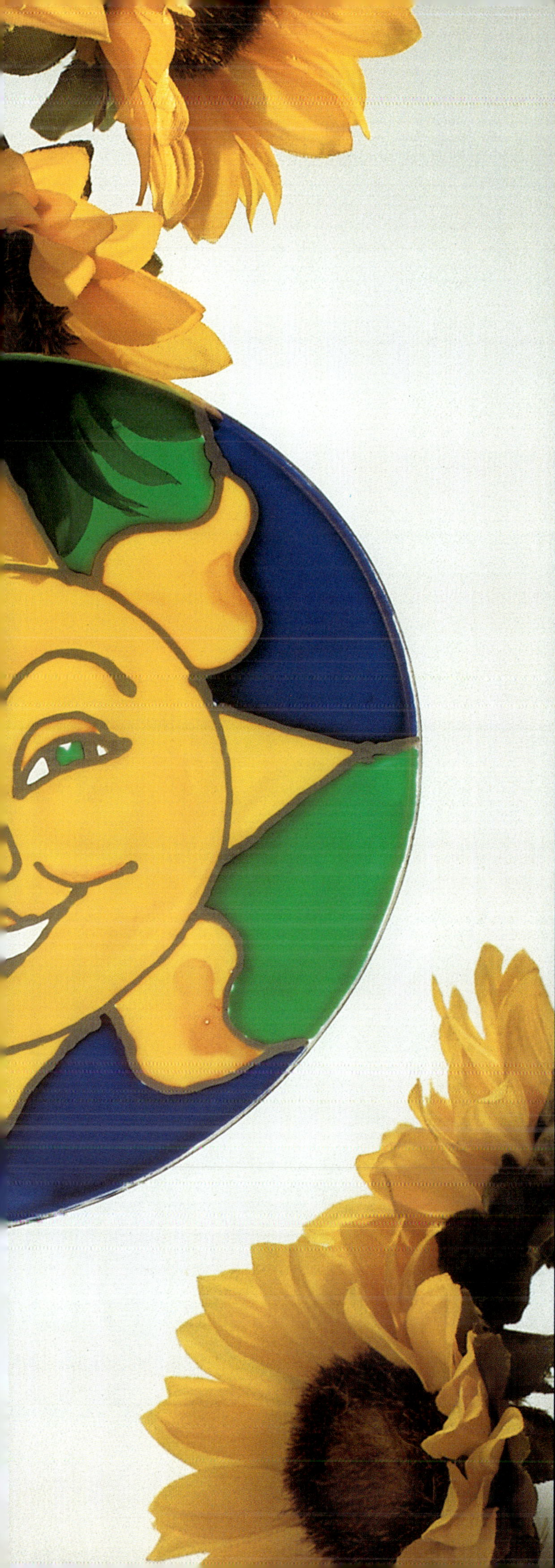

GLASS
PAINTING

These three projects are all quickly and easily achievable in just a couple of hours. One of my favourite gifts to give are the small glass boxes. I often glass paint a vase to complement my favourite flowers - even a jam jar can be transformed into a pretty container with glass painting. Finally, even on the glummest winter's day a colourful suncatcher placed in a light window will bring what sunshine there is dancing into your home. All three ideas are simple but effective designs which I really hope you'll enjoy and that will inspire you to tackle bigger and more ambitious glass painting projects.

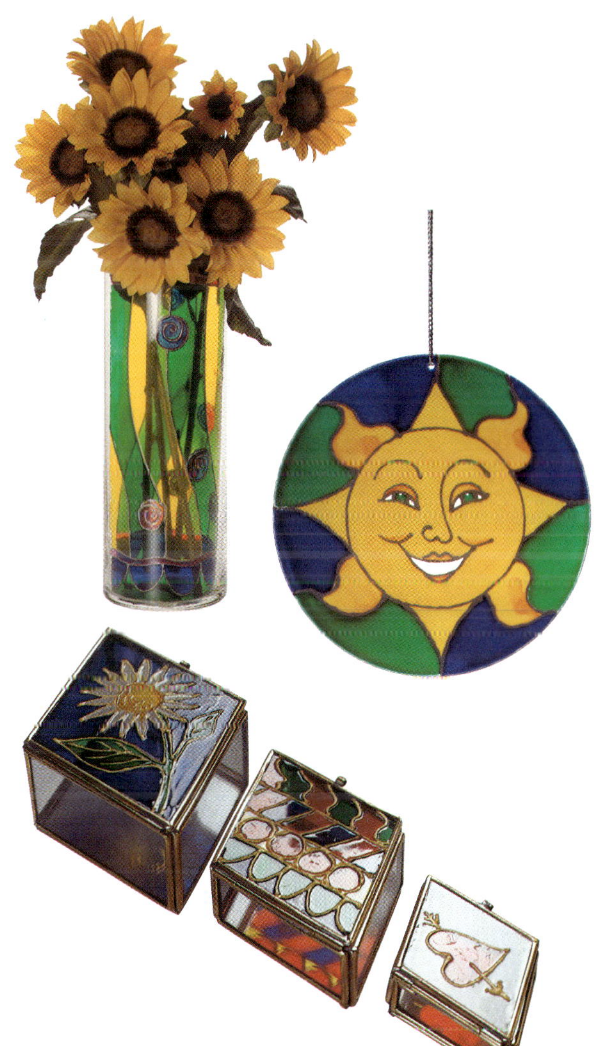

THE ORIGINS OF GLASS PAINTING

Although we might think that mediaeval times saw the birth of glass painting with the wonderful stained and painted glass church windows it was in fact the ancient Egyptians who are recorded as the first to paint glass – with gold!

By the twelfth century the use of enamel on glass was very common all over the world and especially in Europe. These enamel colours were usually baked on.

We are most familiar with painted church windows. The actual artwork was done in dark brown and the glass then fired. A method of painting with silver oxide that produced an amber end effect was called Schwarzlot.

Glass painting was most popular at the end of the eighteenth century when bottles and goblets were painted in cold colours and gold leaf applied. Central Europe has always had the finest reputation for glass painting with both craftsmen and country peasants decorating windows, mirrors and glass objects. It's recorded that by 1860, 380,000 glass paintings were produced in one decade at a Bavarian glass works.

The craft had a real place in the civic and public life of history and many events, styles and fashions are recorded in the pictures painted on glass, yet very little is known about the individual artists. A greater sadness is that so many historical examples have vanished, the nature of the medium is that many works have been broken. Also, of course, with the religious turmoil in mediaeval Europe many monasteries and churches were ransacked and destroyed.

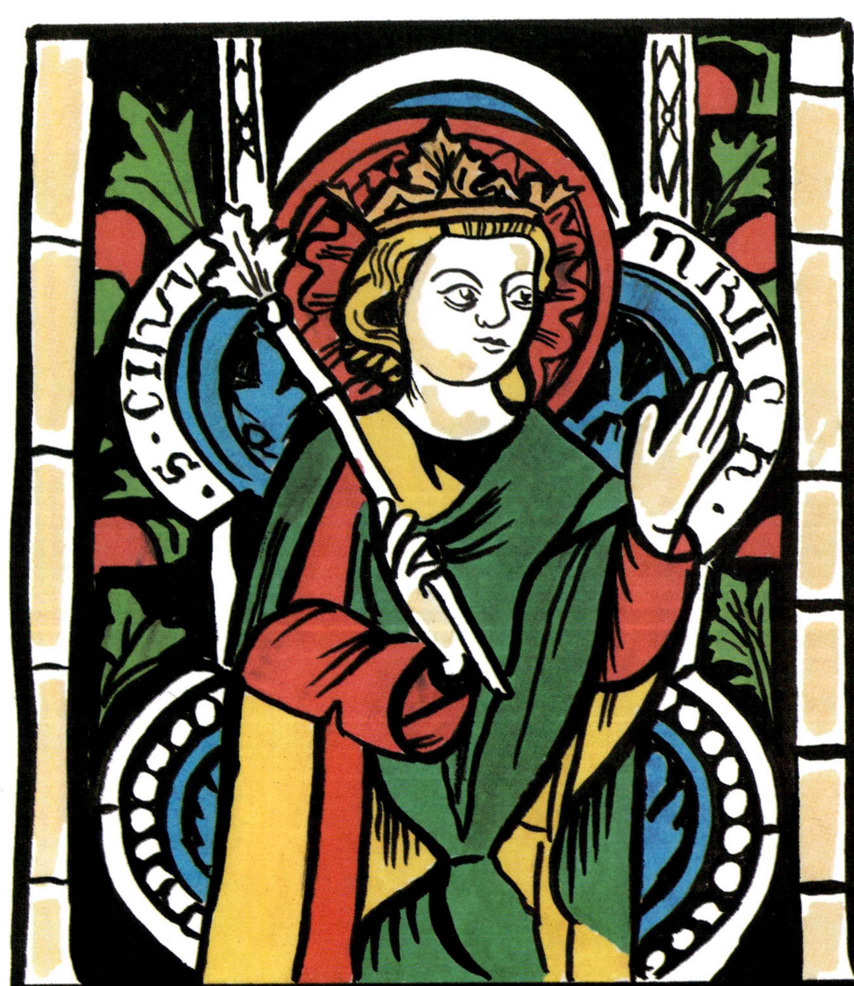

In more recent times decorated glass has found its way into all aspects of life and fashion. Drinking glasses, lamps, mirrors and windows were coloured or etched using cold colouring techniques during the nineteenth century. Crafts with glass particularly flourished at the turn of the century during the Art Nouveau period with long flowing lines twining into images of flowers, insect wings and vine tendrils particularly effective.

Artists such as Louis Comfort Tiffany and Rene Lalique are famous for their interpretation of art with glass but there were many others who satisfied the Victorian love of combining glass and ornamentation. This age also loved to decorate the most utilitarian of items and glass painting came into its own with the large glassed-in window boxes which became popular to protect plants from city smog. A Dr Nathaniel Bagshaw-Ward was fed up because his collection of ferns perished outside his London home and equally suffered inside from the fumes of the oil and gas lamps. So he devised a glassed-in window box that provided a microclimate for his plants. Artists decorated the lower part of it with paintings so it became an attractive addition to the house as well as having a practical purpose. Today, decorated glass is still popular and very much part of our heritage.

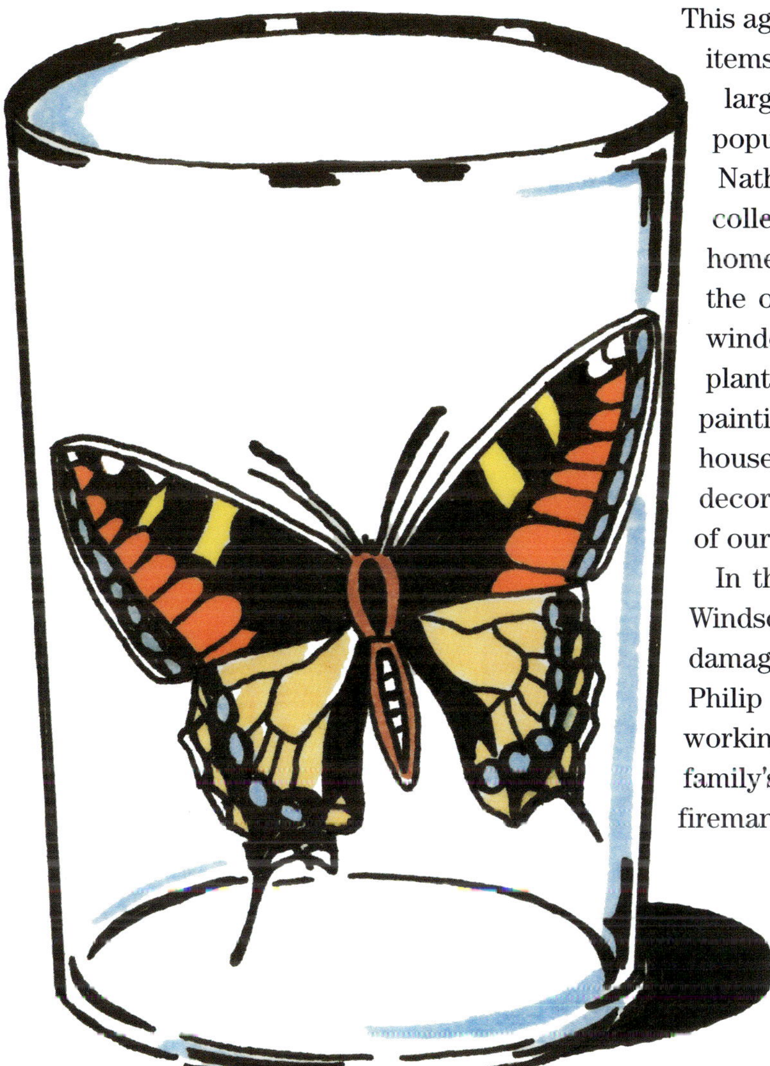

In the late 1990s it featured in the restoration of Windsor Castle after the fire that caused so much damage in 1992. The Duke of Edinburgh, Prince Philip expressly asked designer Joseph Nutjens, working on the stained glass window in the Royal family's private chapel, to include the image of a fireman with his hose fighting to extinguish the blaze.

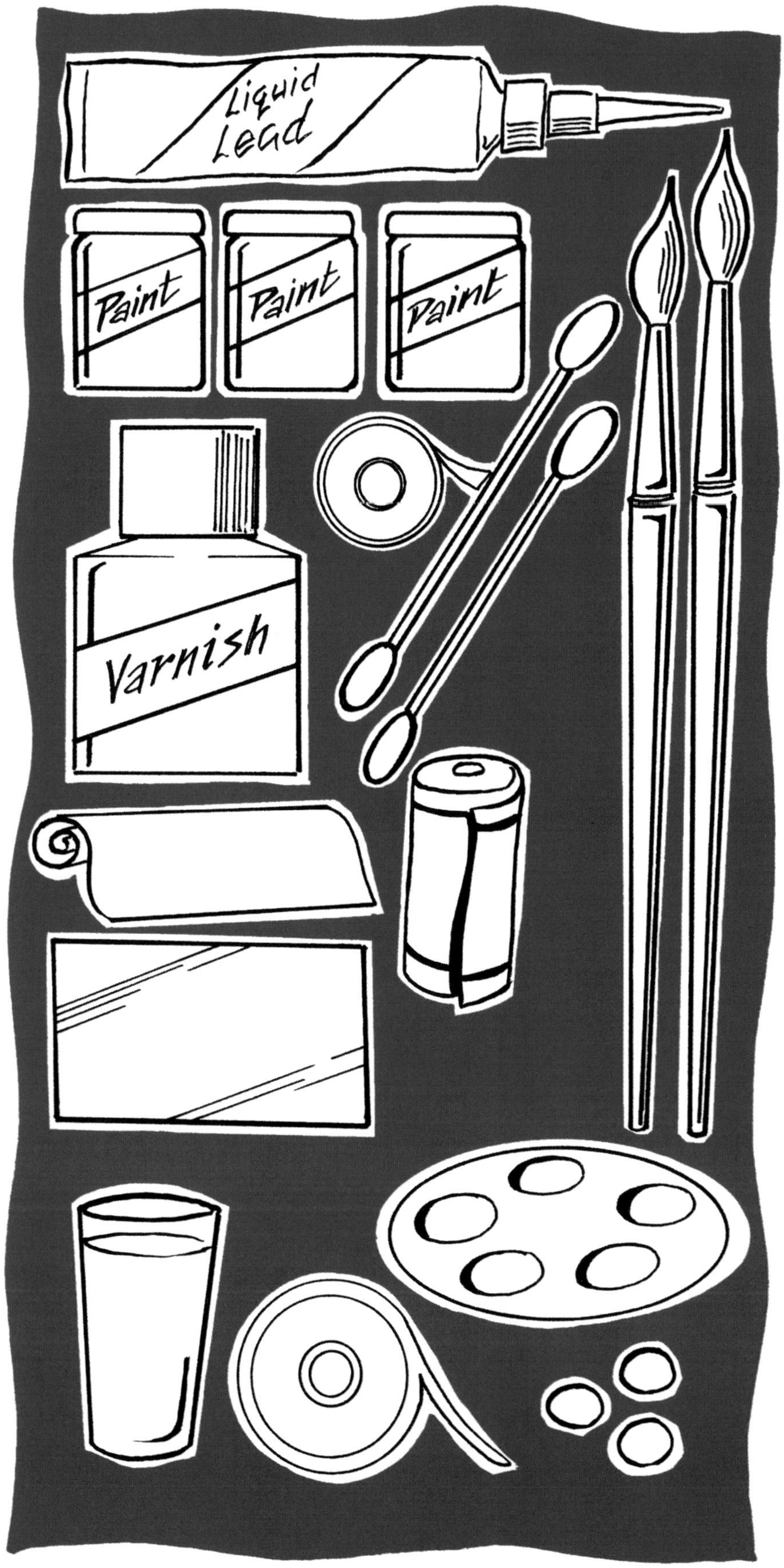

Liquid lead

Paint

Tape

Cotton buds

Brushes

Varnish

Pattern

Glass, acetate or plastic

Kitchen roll

Palette

Beads

Lead strip

Water

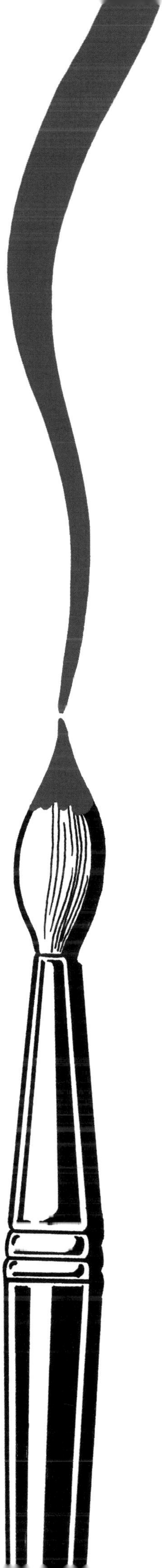

EQUIPMENT

You can begin to glass paint with very basic equipment. First of all, of course, you need some transparent surface to paint on and while **glass** is cheap and readily available don't rule out clear plastic and acetate. There are lots of glass shapes available from craft shops and your home will probably be full of plain glass items. If you want to paint a pane of glass you must paint it when it is flat.

Liquid lead is a thick paste that you buy in tubes in various metallic colours. You can fix a gutta nib onto the nozzle which will let you draw finer lines. You squeeze it straight from the tube. You can also buy peel-off leading and a special self-adhesive lead strip.

It helps to stick your **pattern** down under your glass with **tape** to keep it straight.

The **paint** you use for glass is especially transparent although you can also buy opaque black and white paints. They will be either water-based or solvent-based. You can't mix the two and I recommend the beginner use water-based. Read the manufacturer's instructions carefully for thinning the paints and cleaning your brushes.

You will need to keep the colours separate so a **palette** is a good idea and it's important to use good quality sable or fine white nylon **brushes** with a good tip that will allow you to get right into awkward corners. Mistakes can be corrected with **cotton buds** or **kitchen roll.**

You can decorate your glass further by sticking on **glass beads** and painting around them.

You can buy a special **varnish** to paint over and protect your finished glass painting.

Ventilation is a very important safety consideration if you are using the solvent-based paints so make sure you work in a room with a window open or even better work outside if the weather is fine.

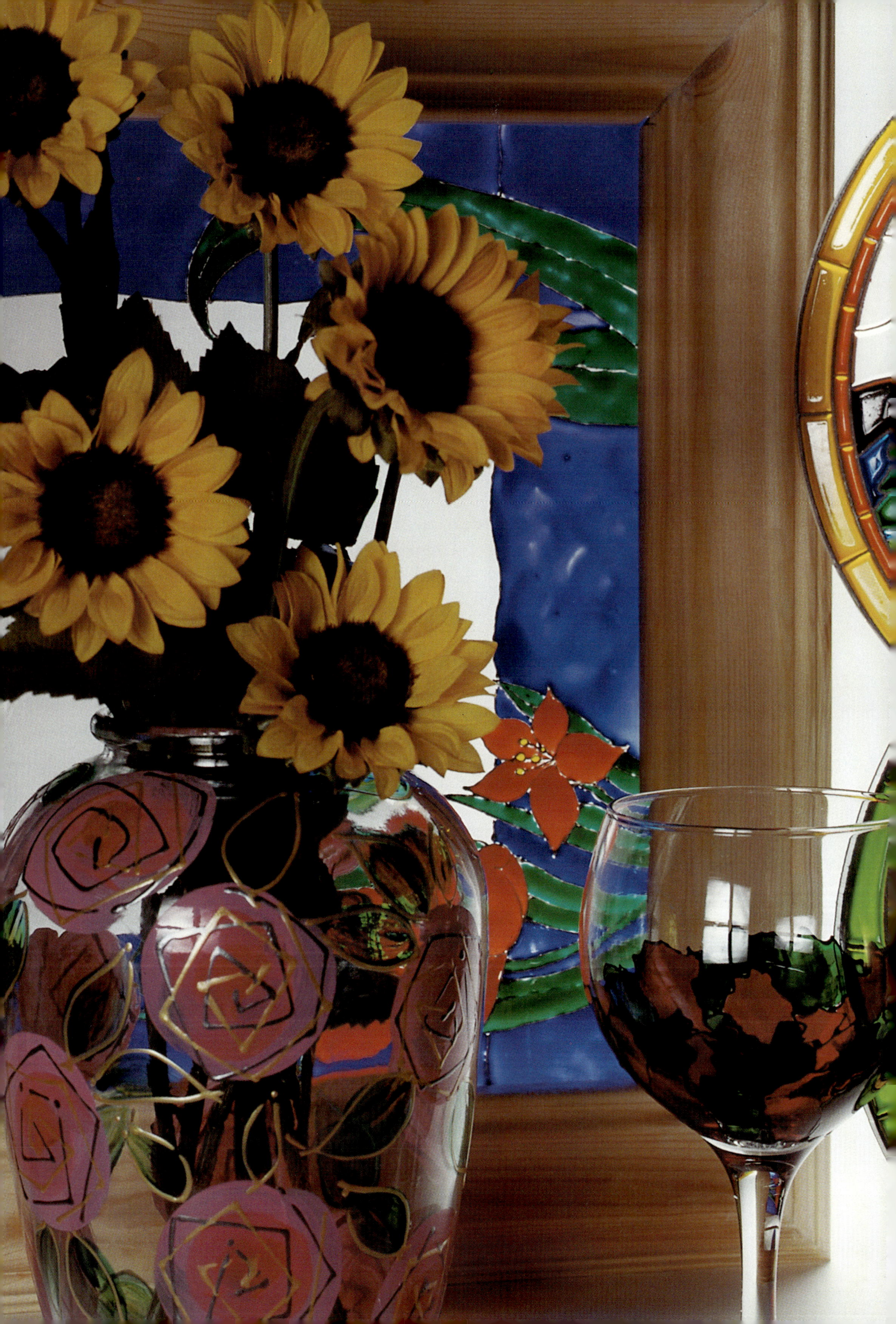

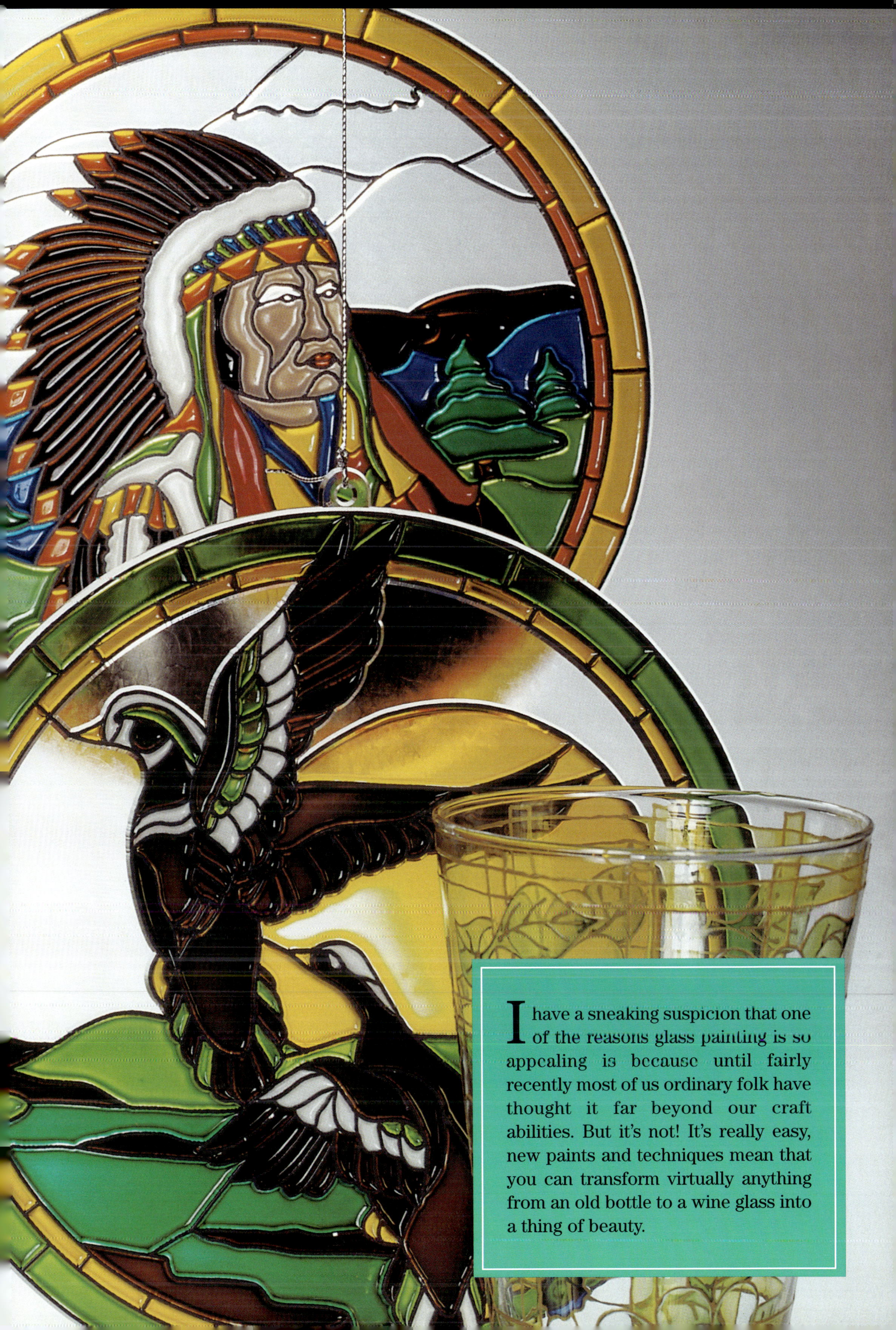

I have a sneaking suspicion that one of the reasons glass painting is so appealing is because until fairly recently most of us ordinary folk have thought it far beyond our craft abilities. But it's not! It's really easy, new paints and techniques mean that you can transform virtually anything from an old bottle to a wine glass into a thing of beauty.

TECHNIQUES

There is a technique to painting on glass and I have to confess it took me a couple of goes to get the hang of it. It's probably best to start off with the water-based paints and practise on a piece of acetate or spare glass.

DAPPLING

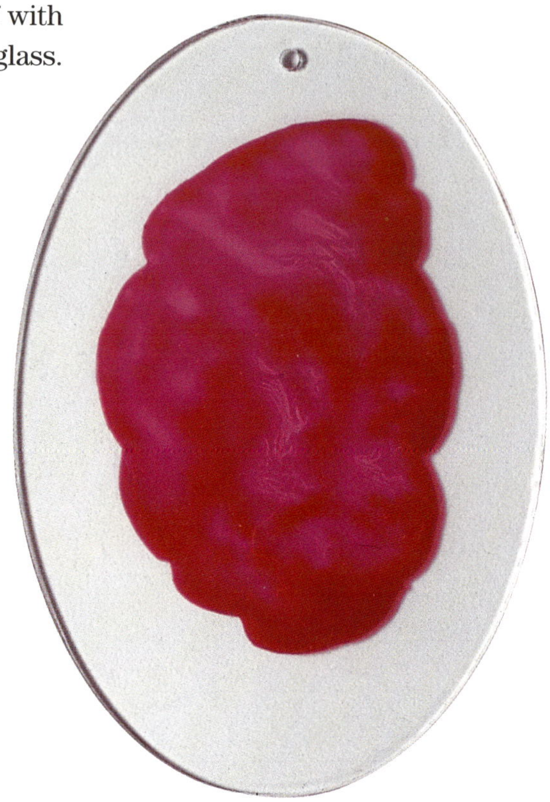

This is a way to add texture to your glass painting. It actually gives your painting an antique look. Paint your area as normal, then dip your brush in either water (if you are using water-based paints) or neat white spirit (if you are using solvent-based paints) and gently drop a few drops onto the paint.

PAINT FLOW BLENDING

This will produce a clouded effect. Using the opaque colours paint over the area, then very lightly dip your brush into other colours, touch the opaque area and gently pull and tease the colour through. This is excellent for shading.

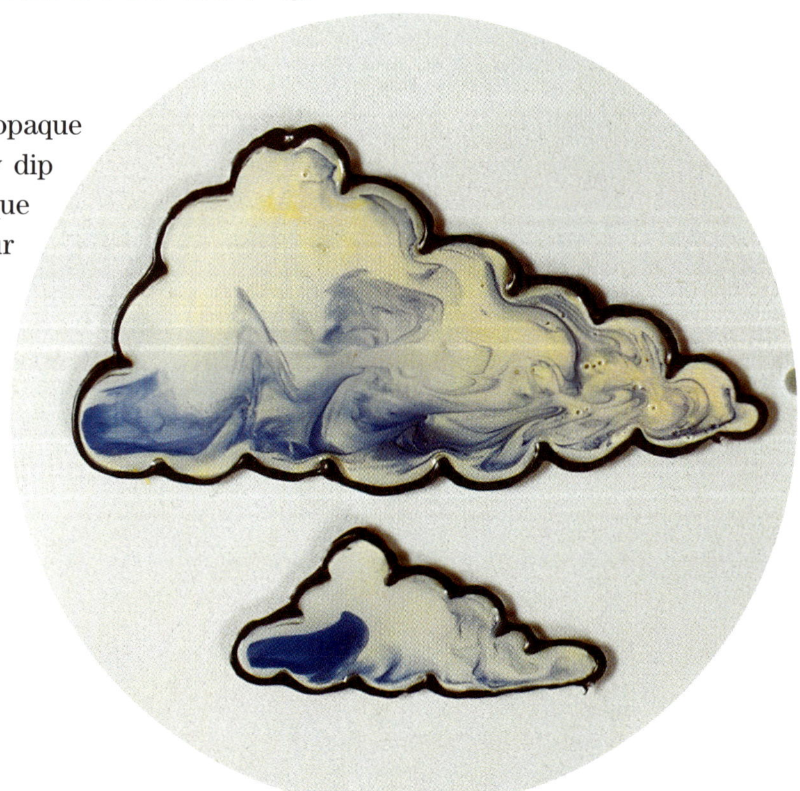

DECORATION

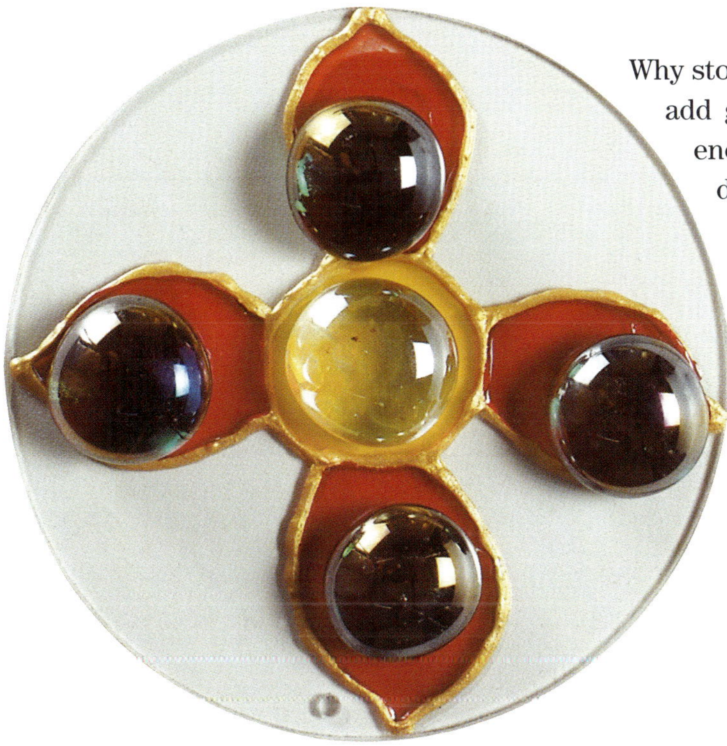

Why stop at just paint to decorate your glass item? Why not add glass beads or other jewels? Make sure you leave enough space when doing the leading and I suggest you do any painting first. Then a dab of glue and you've added even more interest to your transformation!

LEADING

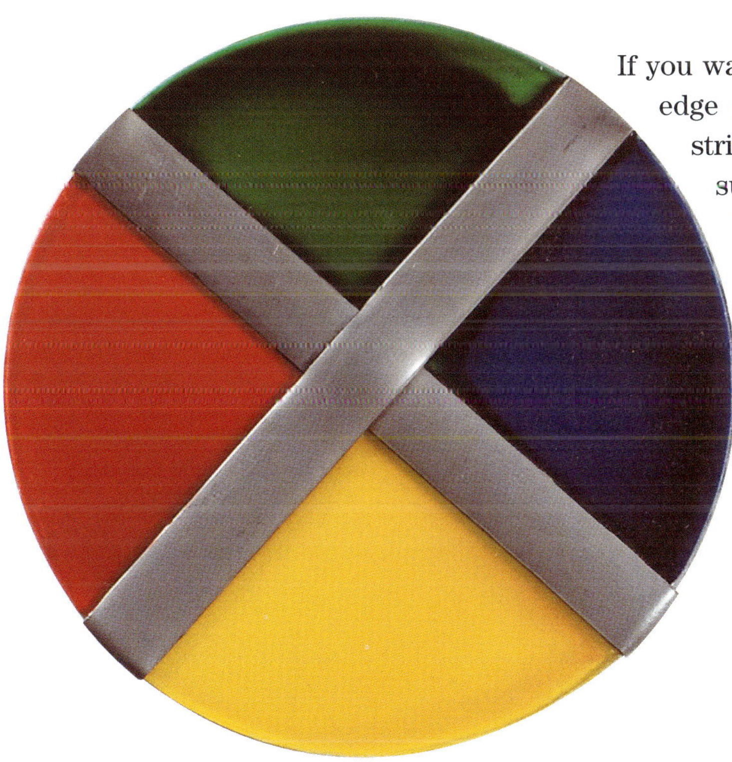

If you want to go for the full authentic look you can edge your work with peel-off self-adhesive lead strip or use it to separate your colours. Make sure that the surface of the glass is grease-free before applying the lead and you will need scissors or a craft knife to cut lengths and go around corners. You can buy lead strip in a roll in various thicknesses from most good craft shops and DIY stores.

STEP-BY-STEP

Always work from the top left corner and be careful not to rest your wrist on the glass. Have some cotton buds or tissues at hand so you can immediately rectify mistakes by wiping them off. As long as you are using water-based colours experiment with mixing them before you start painting your item.

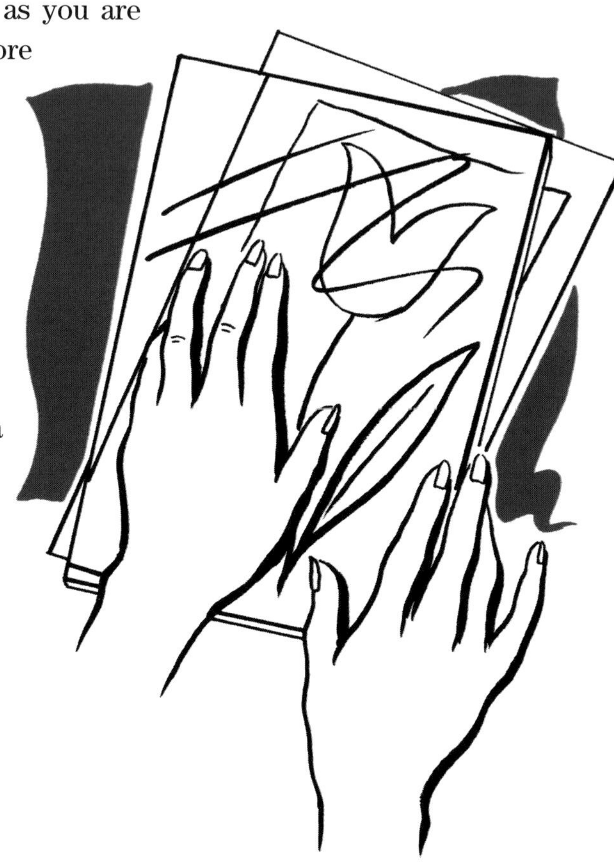

THE PATTERN

It really helps to have a pattern to follow for your lead. On a flat surface place your transparent surface over your chosen pattern and lightly rest the nozzle of the opened liquid lead on top of the line.

THE LIQUID LEAD

Applying even pressure, gently squeeze the tube, tracing over the lines. Squeeze from the bottom which will make the tube easier to hold and stop air getting in which might cause spluttering. Make sure you leave no gaps in the lines or at joins and leave to dry. Depending on how thickly you have painted this can take anything from 30 minutes to 3 hours.

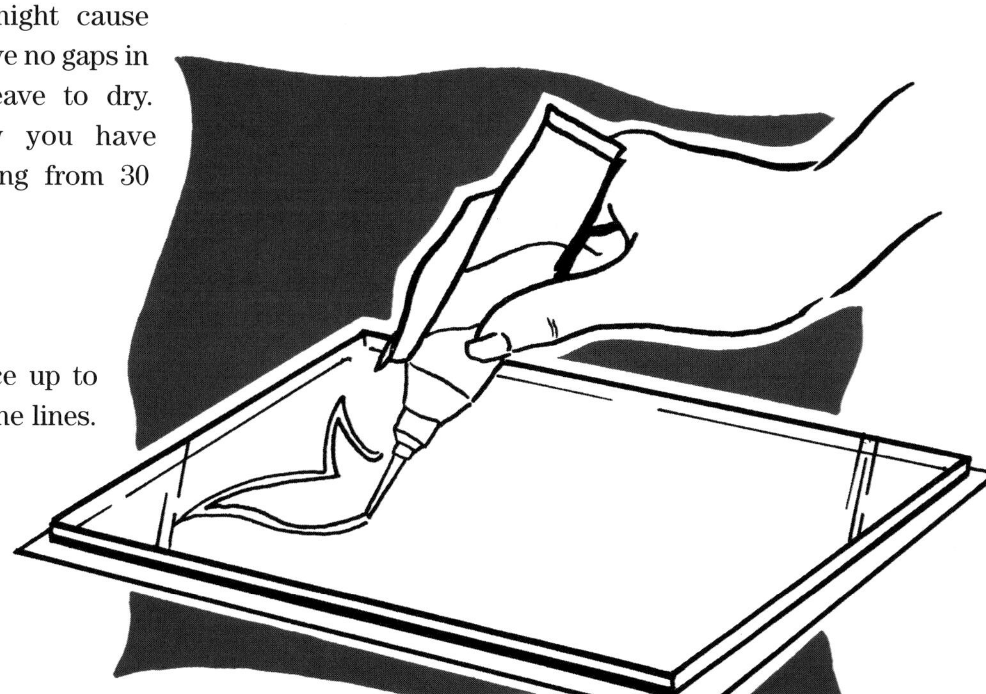

Checking the outline

I always hold my leaded piece up to the light to check for gaps in the lines.

PAINTING

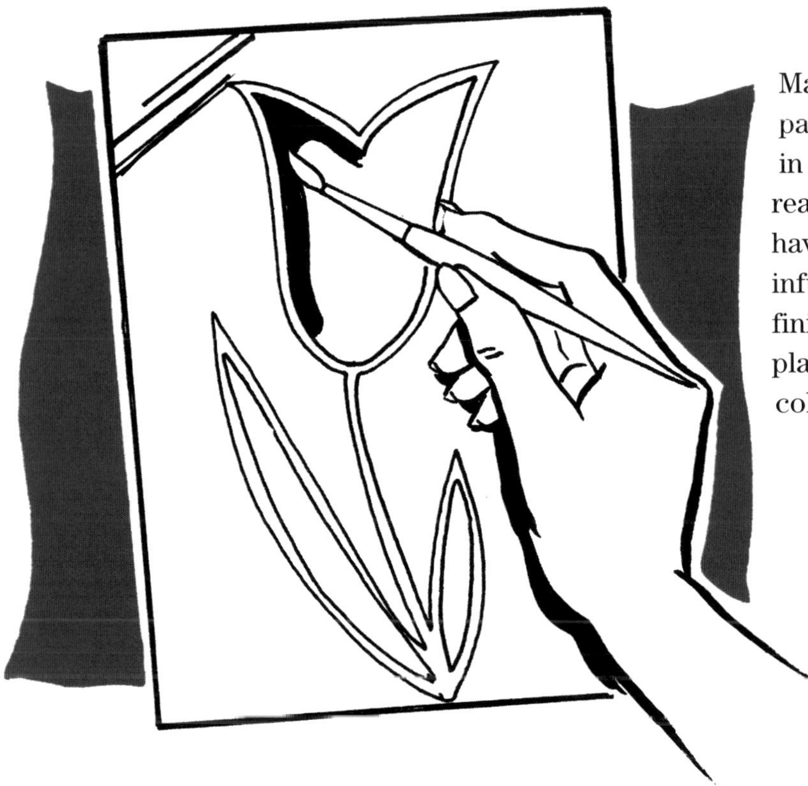

Make sure your brush is well charged with paint and working with one colour at a time fill in the areas pushing the paint out to the lead to really fill in every gap. Especially make sure you have filled all the corners up - it is absolutely infuriating to hold your piece up when it's finished and see light glinting through in odd places. Clean your brush thoroughly between colour changes.

VARNISHING

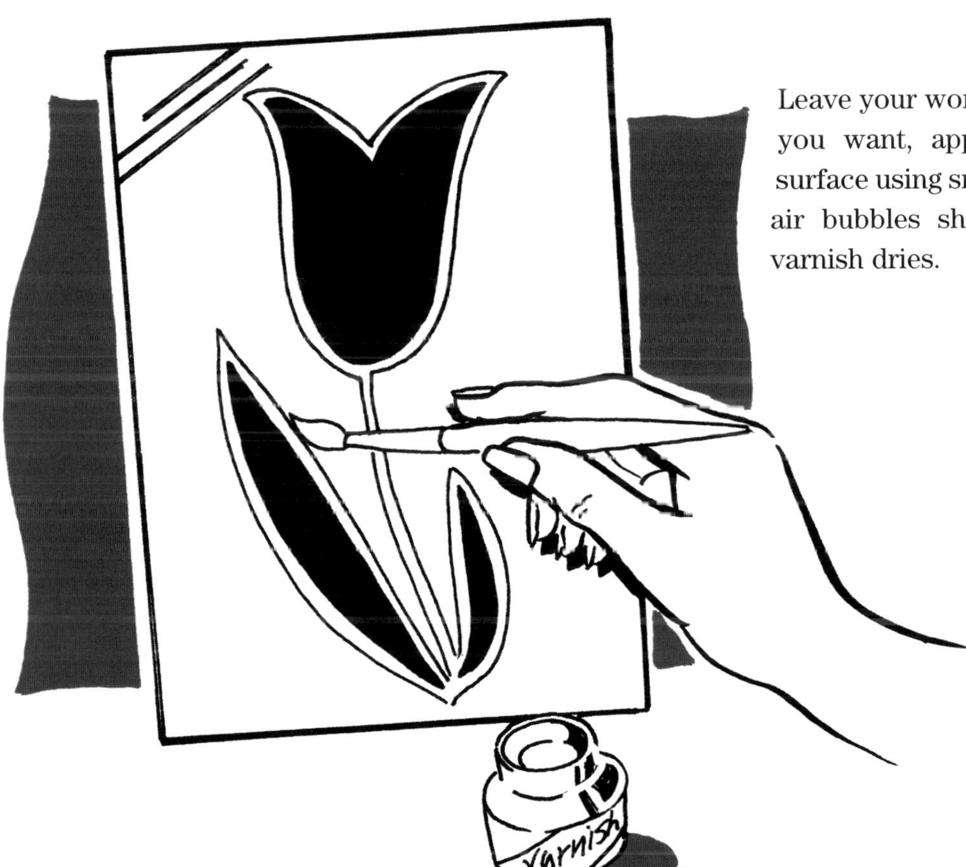

Leave your work on a flat surface to dry. Then, if you want, apply protective varnish over the surface using smooth steady brush strokes. Small air bubbles should disappear naturally as the varnish dries.

PATTERN

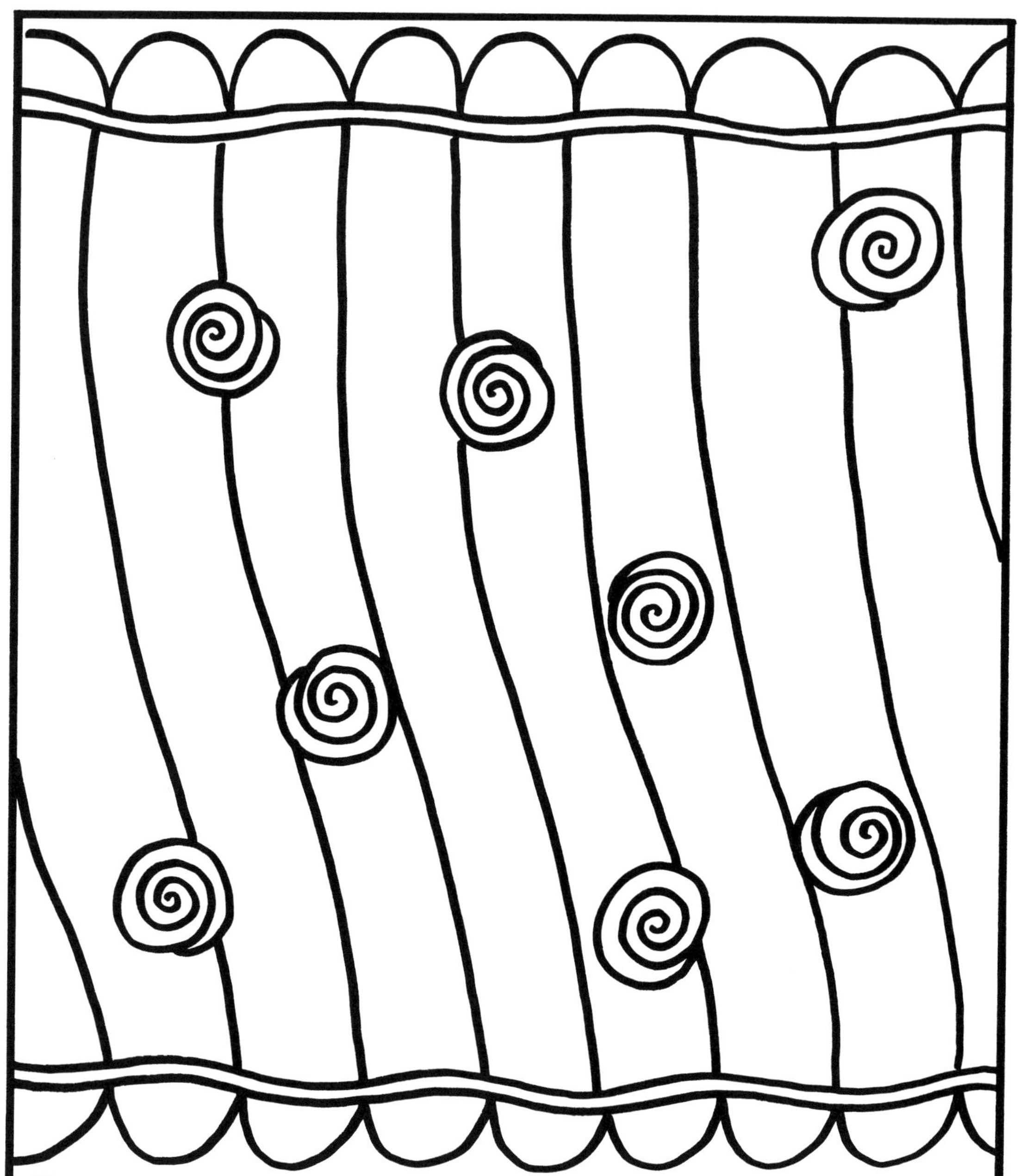

YOU WILL NEED

- Silver liquid lead
- Blue, green, yellow and red glass paints
- A glass vase
- Varnish

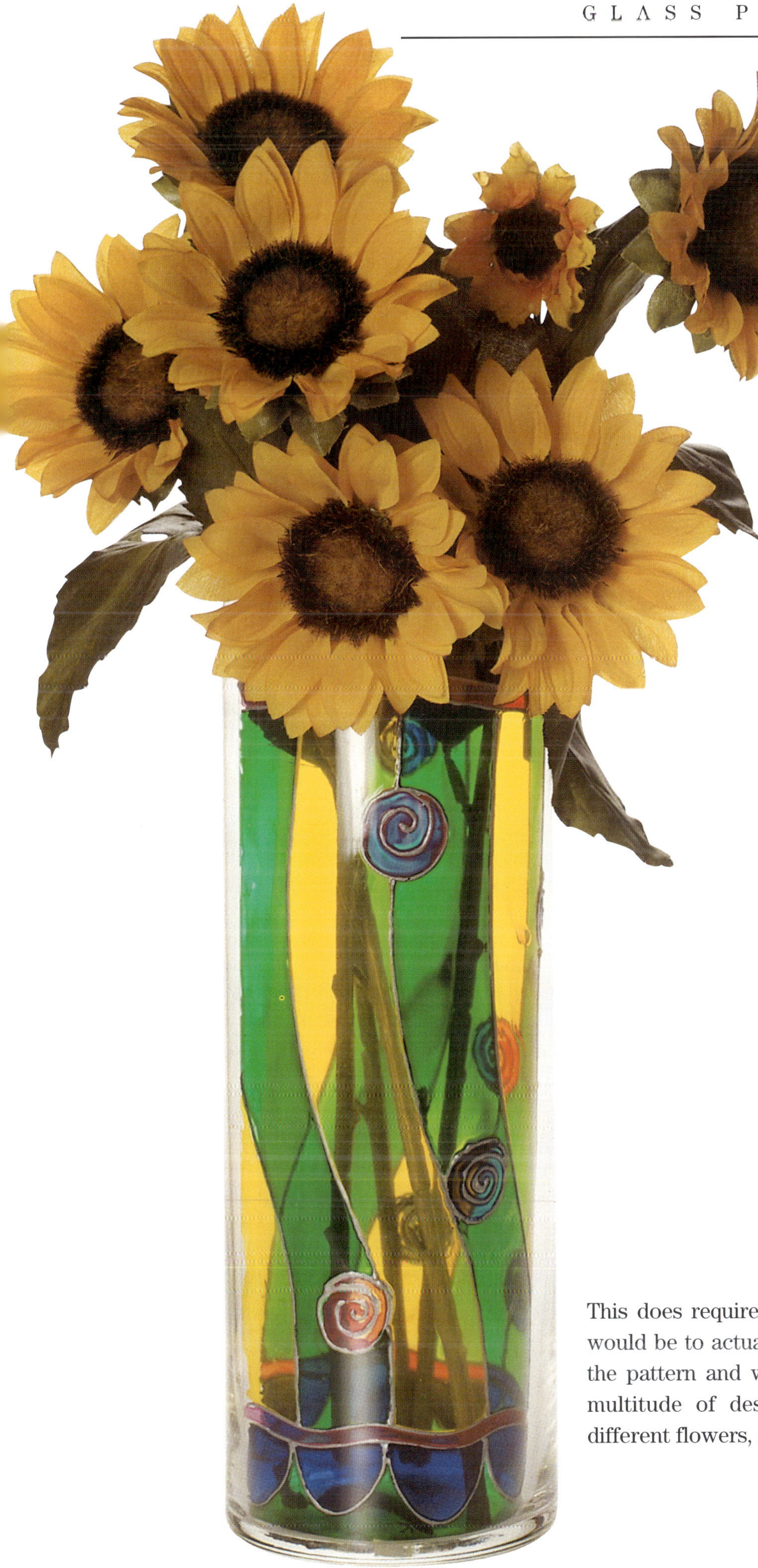

This does require patience to do - an effective cheat would be to actually paint a flat piece of acetate with the pattern and wrap it around... then you can do a multitude of designs to suit different rooms and different flowers, all with one vase.

PATTERN

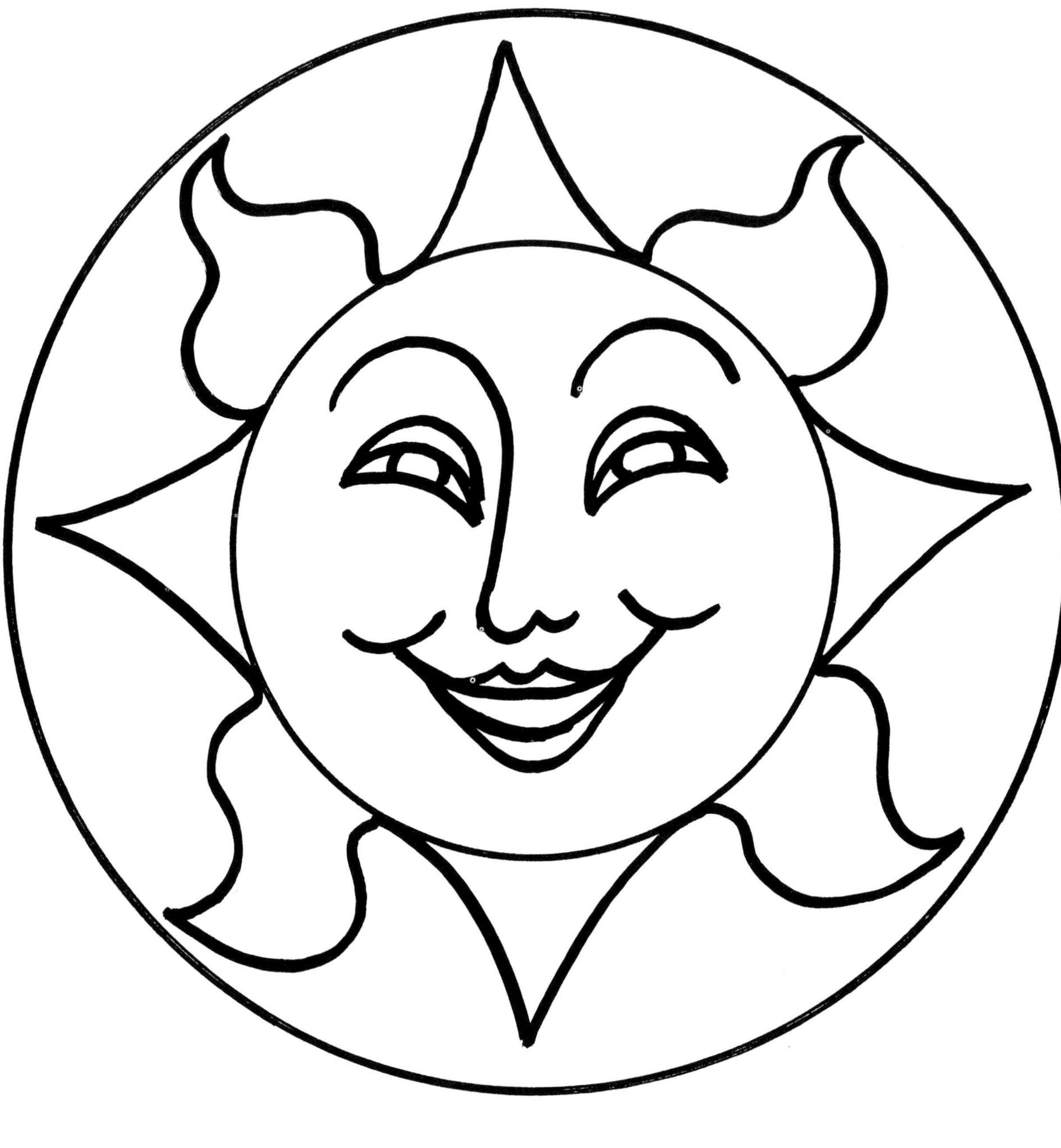

YOU WILL NEED

- Glass or plastic suncatcher to fit pattern with a hole
- Gold liquid lead
- Yellow, blue and green glass paints
- Varnish
- A metre of ribbon

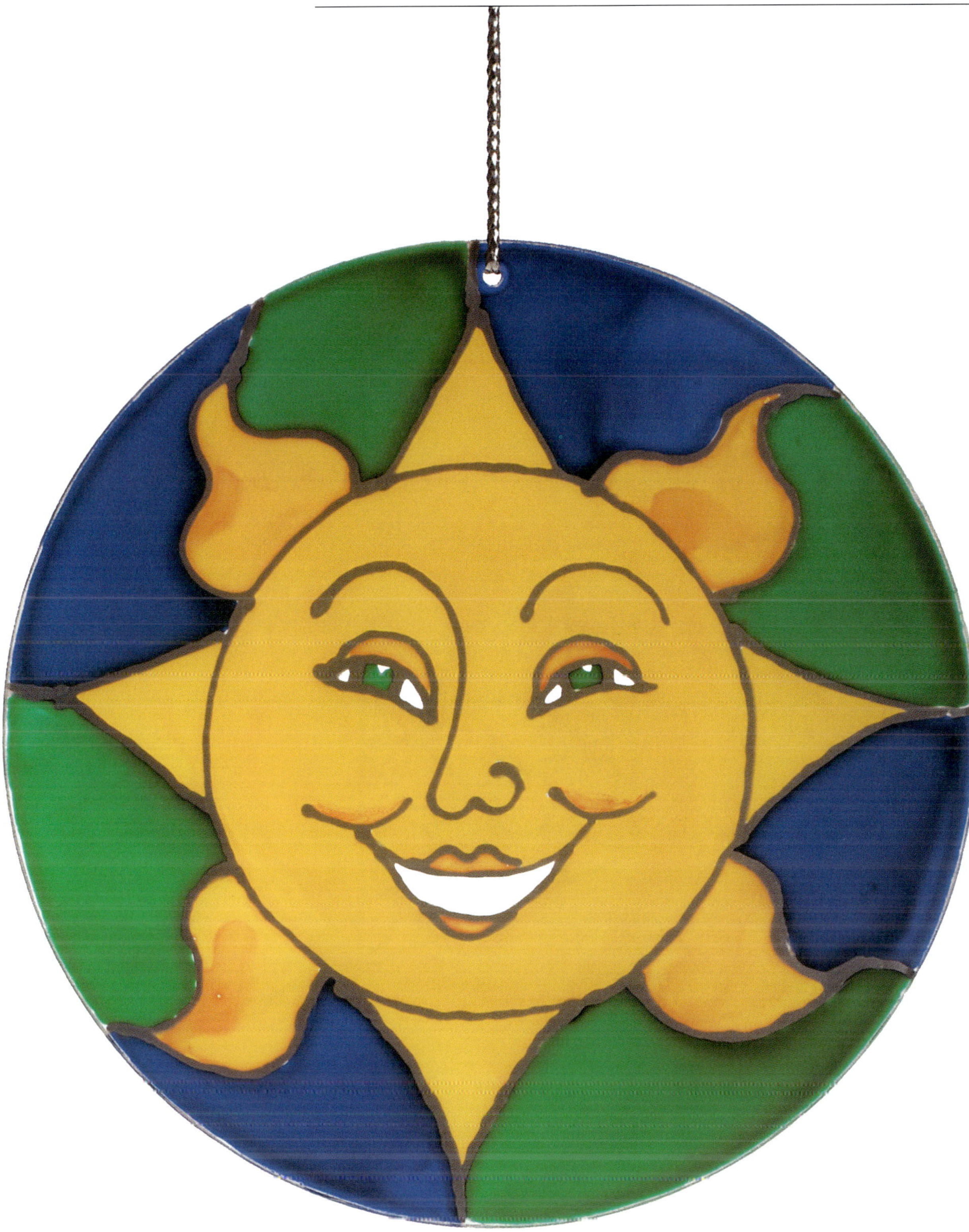

You just can't go wrong with a suncatcher - it will be easy and fun to do and then you can hang it in your window with the ribbon to brighten up every day.

PATTERN

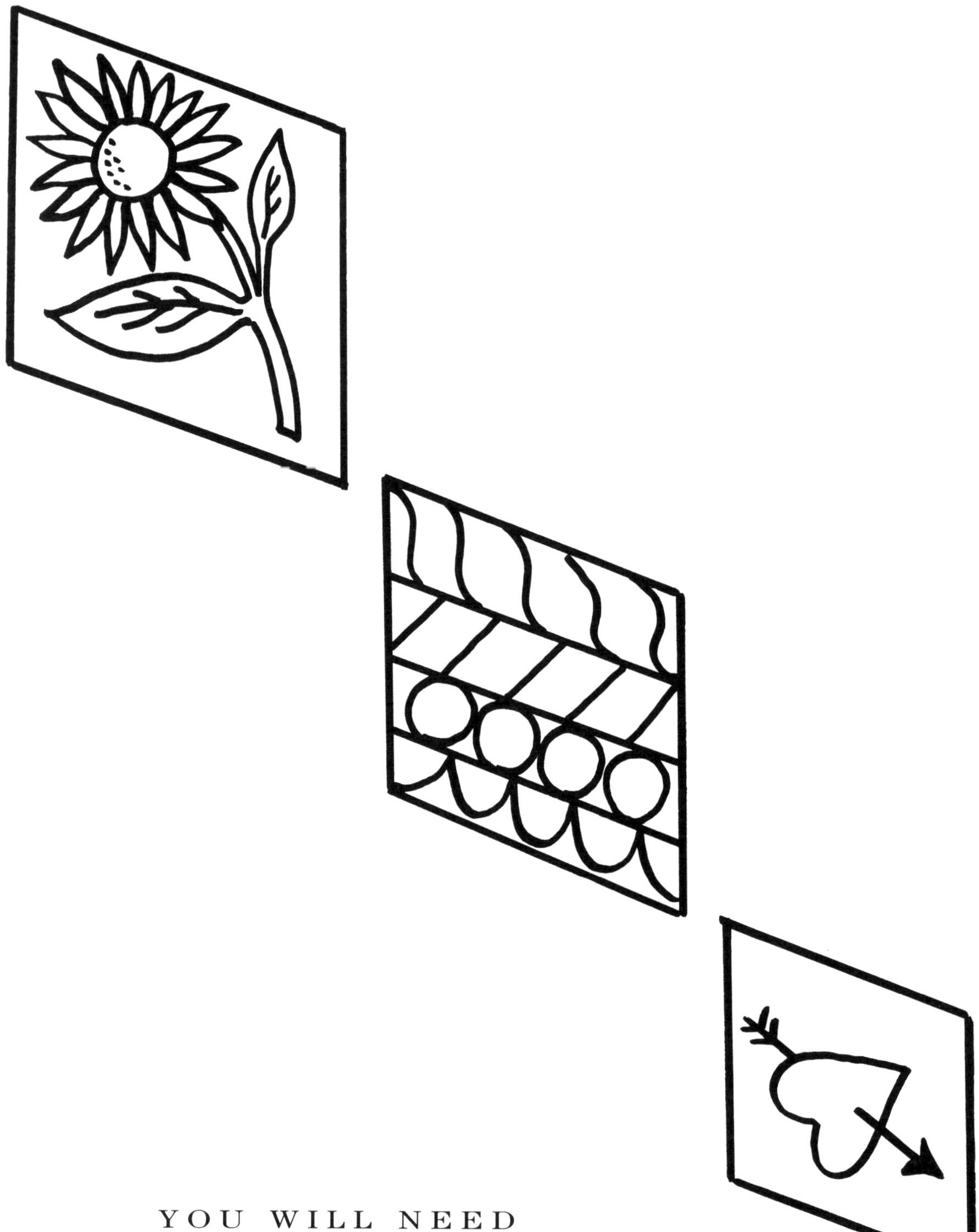

YOU WILL NEED

- Glass boxes
- Gold liquid lead
- Opaque white, yellow, blue, green and red glass paint
- Varnish

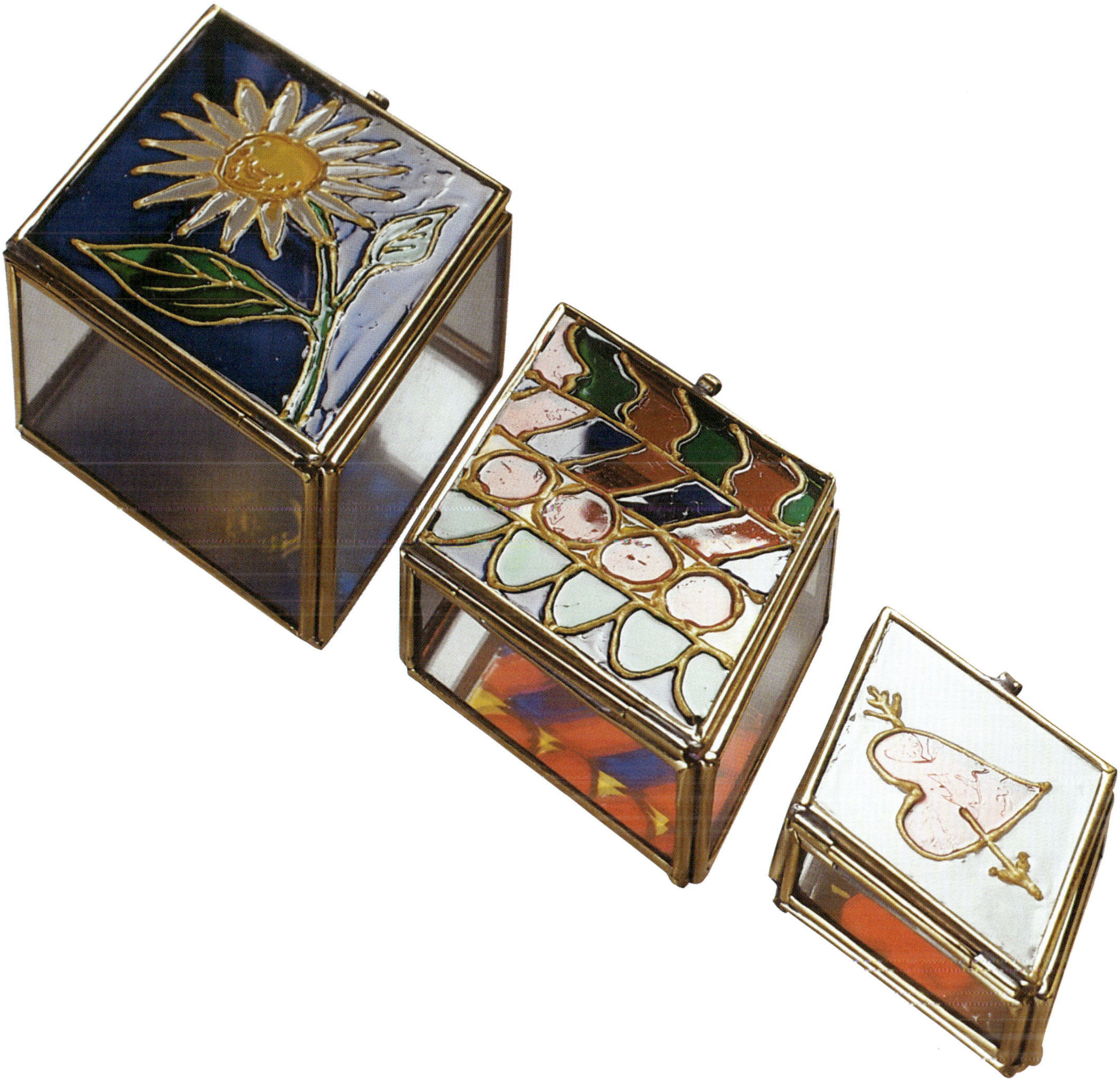

These are just the loveliest presents to make and give and because they have a small area and are flat...you can't really go wrong.

DON'T STOP THERE!

Just look around your home and you'll be amazed how many glass items you have - from windows, to jam jars to mirrors. I bet hardly any of them will be decorated - they're just waiting for you to transform them!

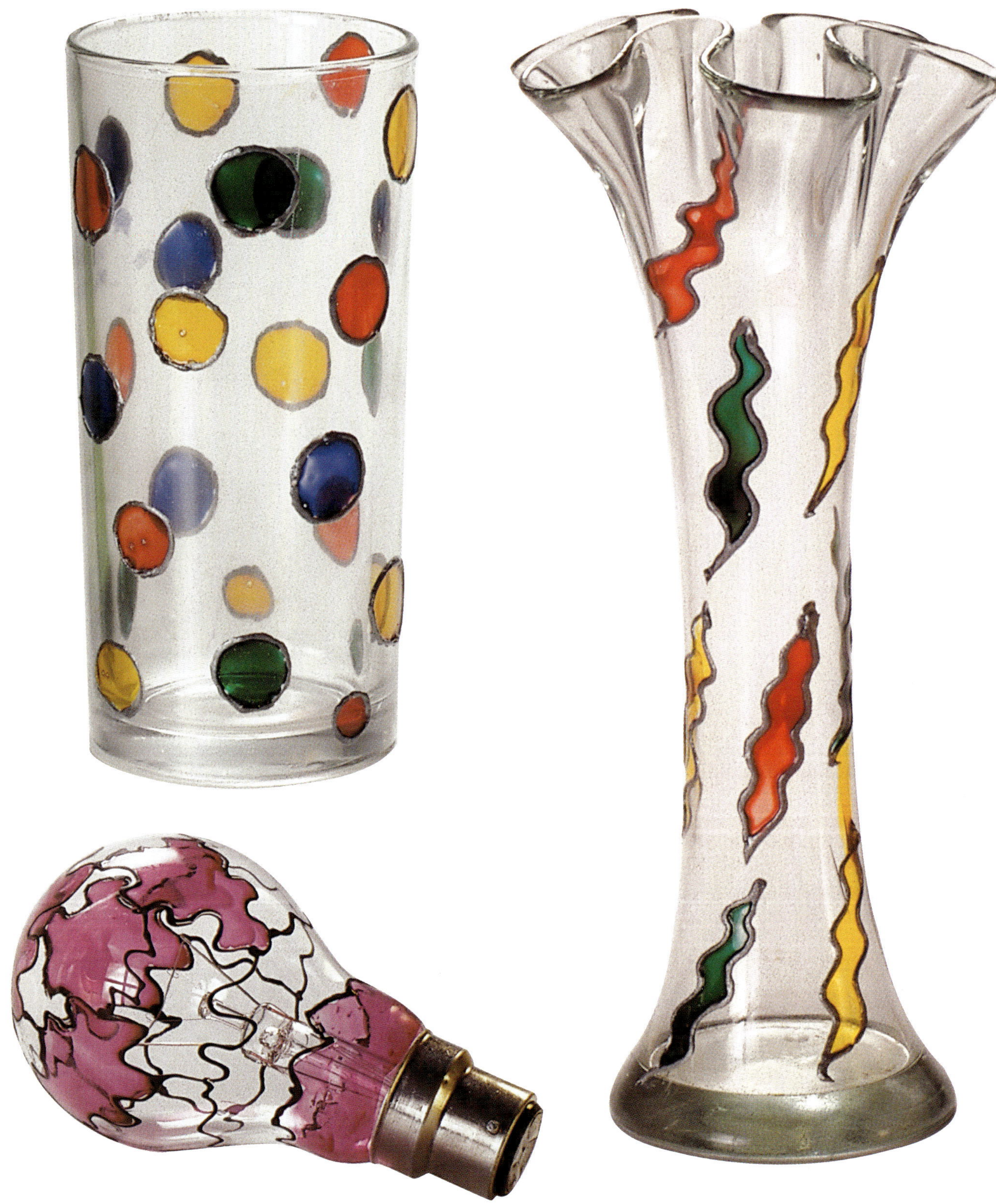

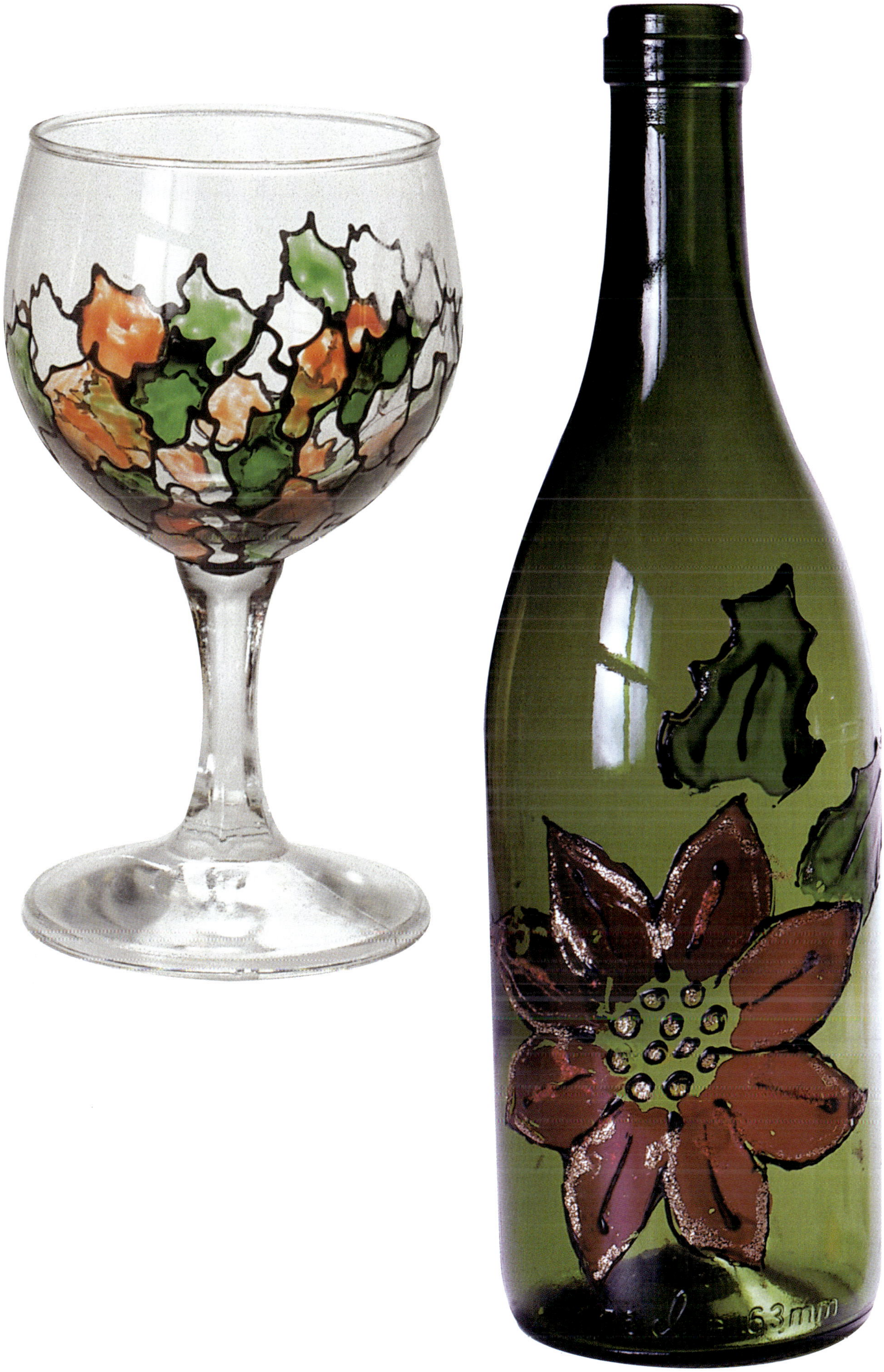

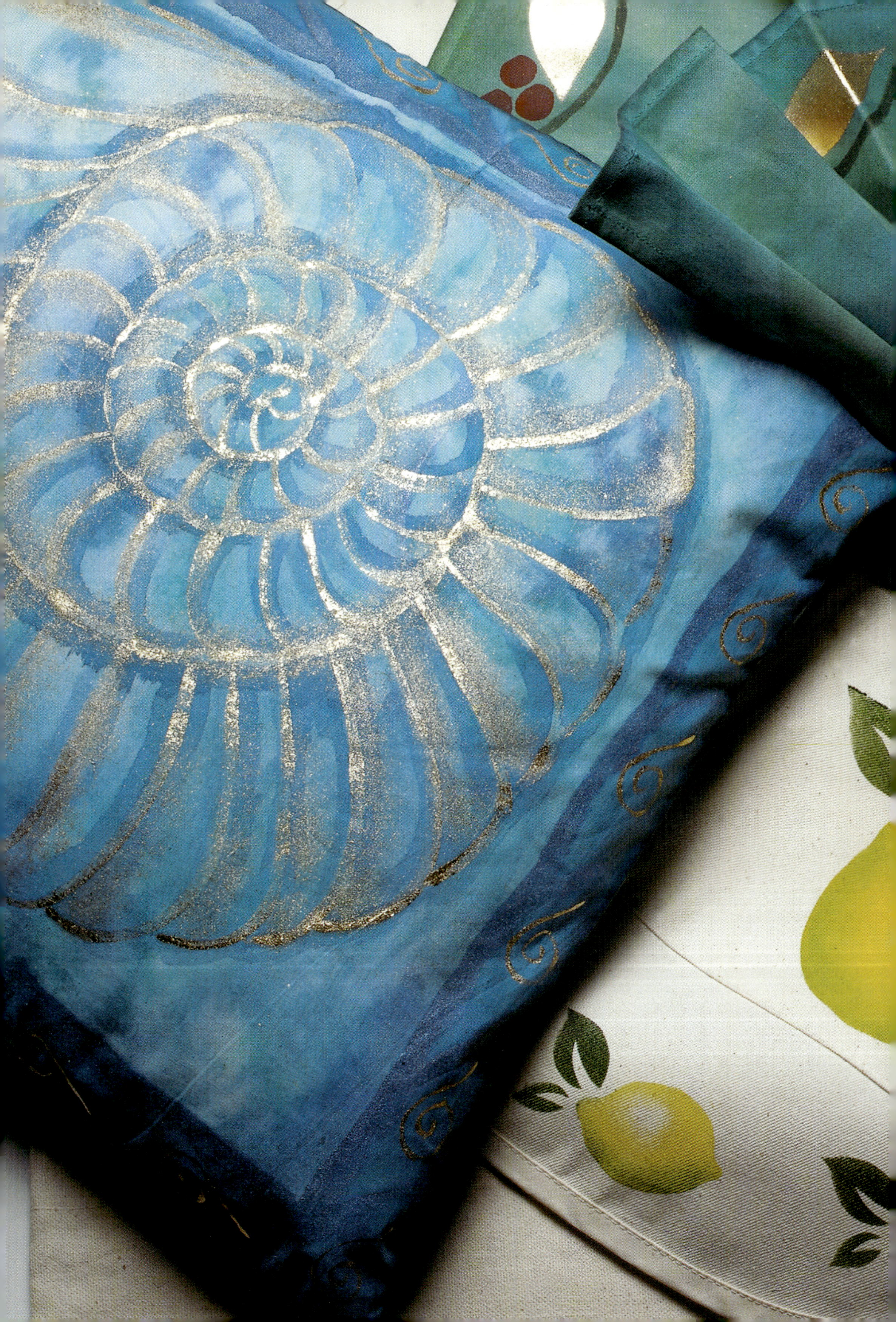

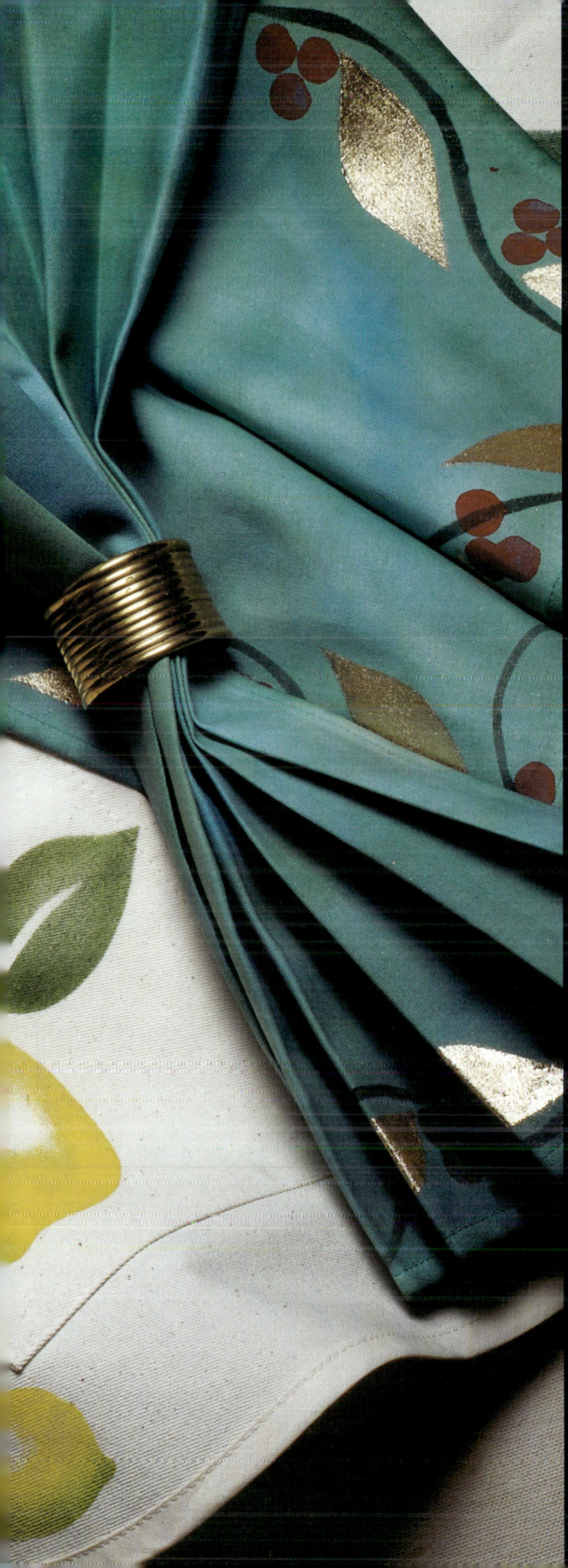

FABRIC
PAINTING

I think you can have more fun with fabric painting than with almost any other craft. Fabric paints are so versatile. You can paint freestyle, you can stamp, sponge or stencil. My three projects will enable you to have a go at all the techniques and you'll end up with something beautiful and useful reflecting your own personal style! Have fun.

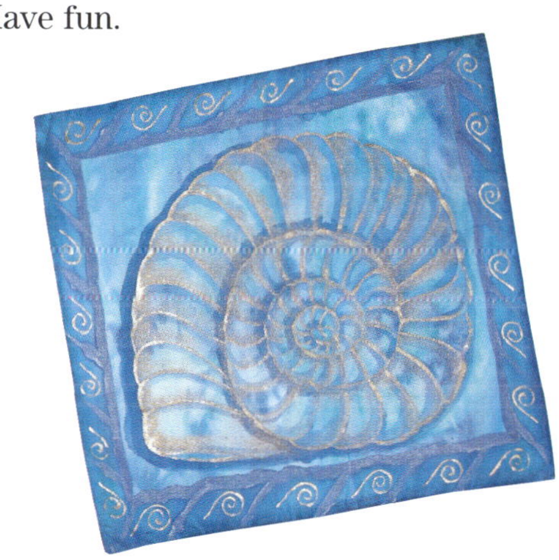

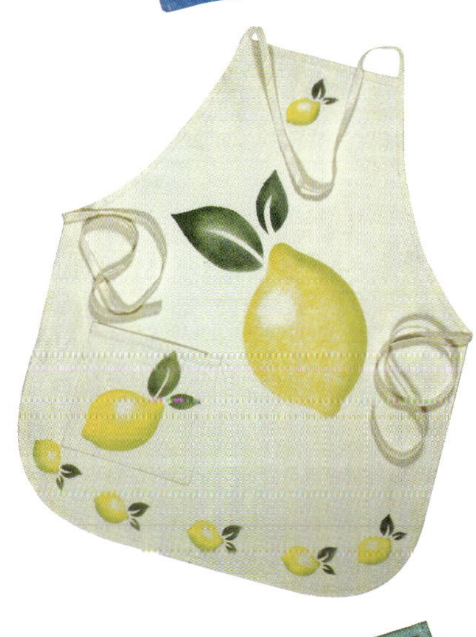

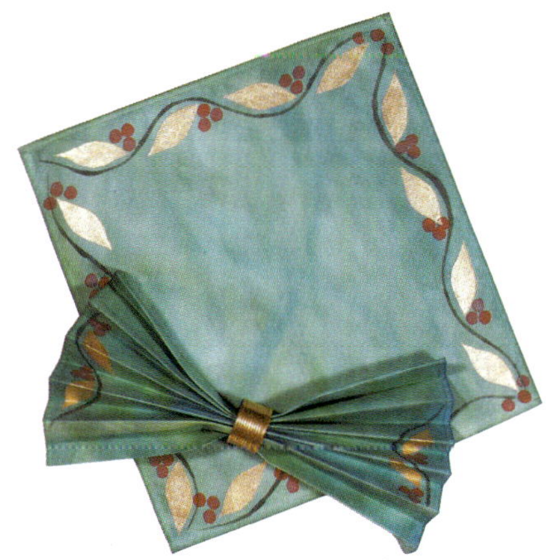

THE ORIGINS OF FABRIC PAINTING

Because of course fabrics are perishable it is quite hard to trace right back to when people first decorated material with paints. We can tell from some cave and wall paintings that fabric painting was a practised craft by about 2000 BC but its origins further back are not known.

We know from tomb drawings that the Egyptians certainly decorated and printed their clothes. Other cultures in India, Indonesia and Java and Peru also appear to have worn clothing which was coloured, probably with colours applied with a brush.

In fact the technique was possibly more akin to resist painting where before dyeing the item would have patterns or designs painted on with a paste or wax that would block the dye from that particular area when it was dipped in the colour.

Block printing and stencil printing are two of the oldest fabric painting techniques that are most relevant to the projects in this book.

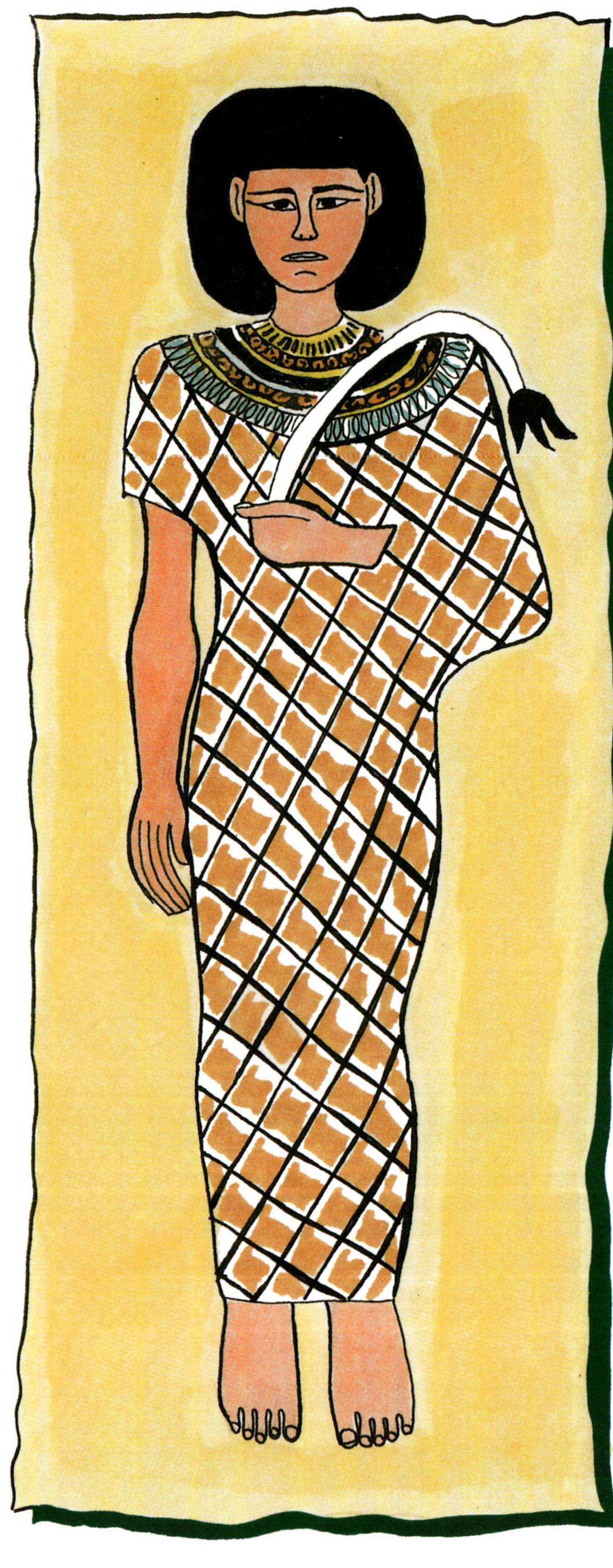

Block printing was probably first used by the ancient Chinese who cut patterns out of one side of a wooden block. They dipped this side into a colour or pigment before pressing it against a textile. If the pattern was to have more than one colour then they would make separate blocks for each colour. The process could take a long time, especially if the pattern was to be repeated over and over again until it covered the whole piece of fabric. The basic principles of block printing are still used today and 'stamping' is a very popular craft for items in the home.

As is stencilling, which also comes from the East - in this case, the Japanese are most commonly known for developing the craft.

Quite simply, as today, they carried out stencil printing by cutting a pattern out of a sheet of card or paper and painting over the cut-out area onto fabric underneath. It couldn't be simpler and probably explains why stencilling's popularity has endured through the centuries.

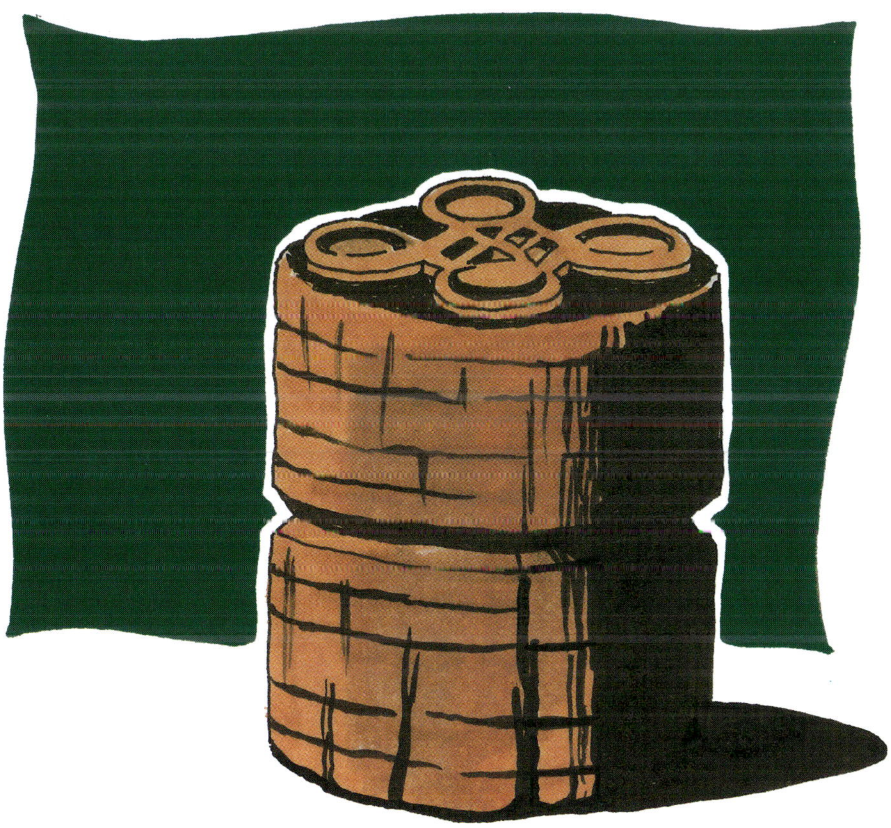

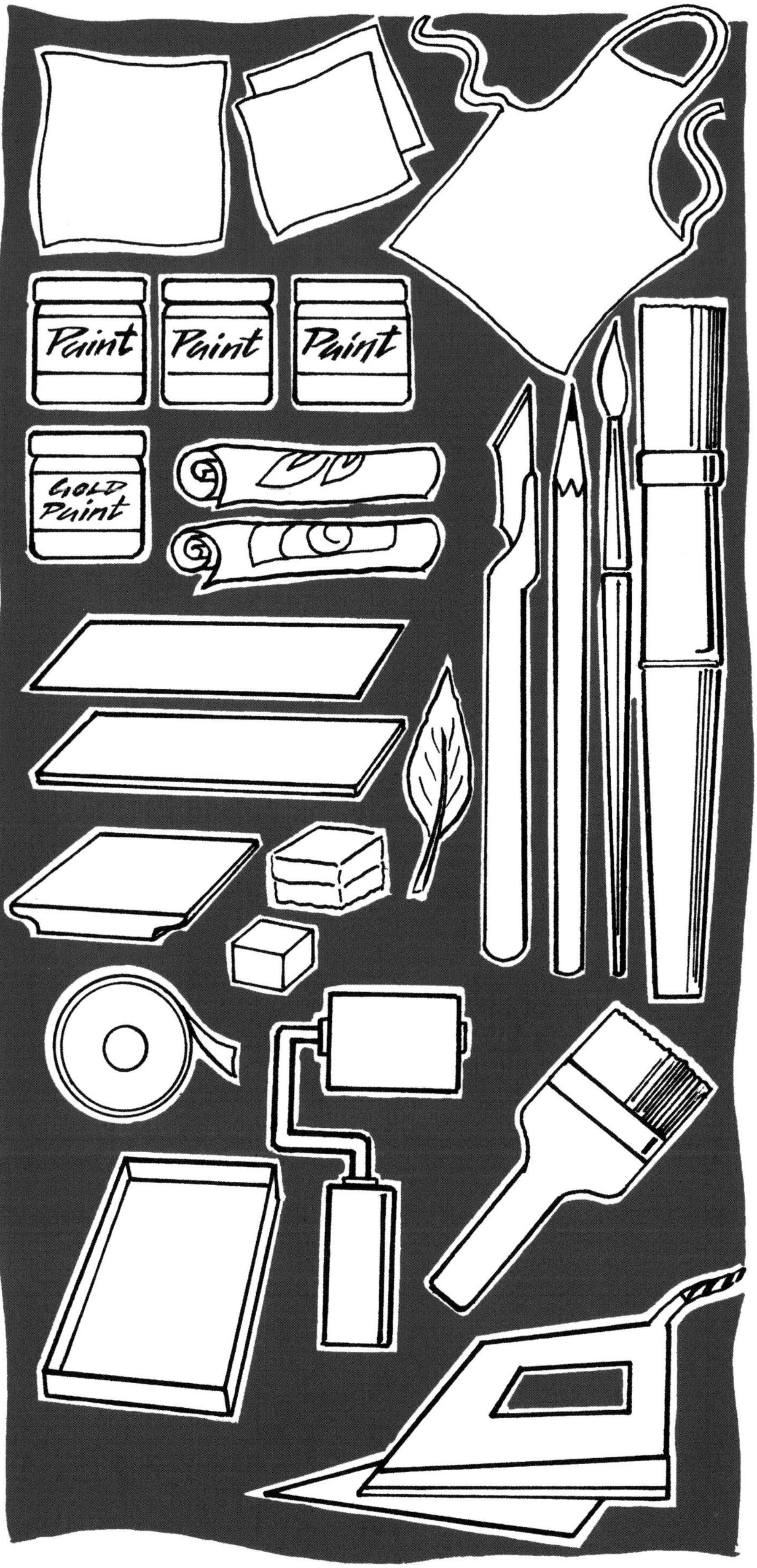

Cushion cover

Napkins

Apron

Paint

Gold paint

Patterns

Stencil card

Sticky back neoprene

Stamp block

Sponge

Stamping cube

Tape

Paint tray

Roller

Leaves etc

Scalpel

Pencil

Brushes

Large brush

Iron

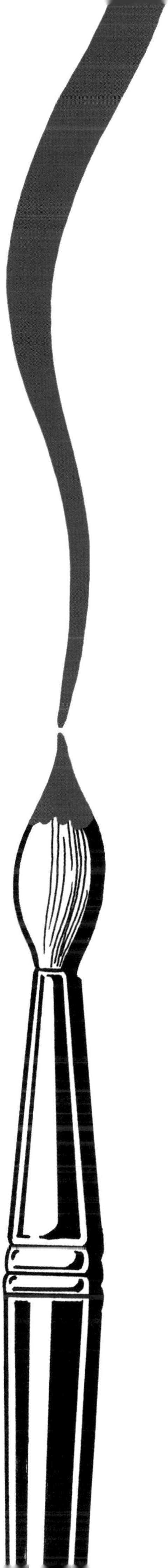

EQUIPMENT

Of course the first thing you need is some blank **fabric** and while I have suggested some items just about anything will do from tea towels to pillowcases. There are lots of **fabric paints** on the market including **gold** and **silver** - I recommend those that are washable after being fixed with an **iron.** Buying blank **stencil card** and **sticky back neoprene rubber** by the square will allow you to cut out your own designs and stick them onto your **stamping blocks** or **finger cubes**.

You will of course then need a **scalpel**.

Any **sponge** will do to get the sponging effect although craft shops do sell clever ones that have different textures.

A couple of **plastic trays**, old ice-cream containers even saucers will be useful as will **brushes** and **rollers** to apply the paint. Plus some basic equipment such as a **pencil**, lots of newspaper and kitchen roll will be useful.

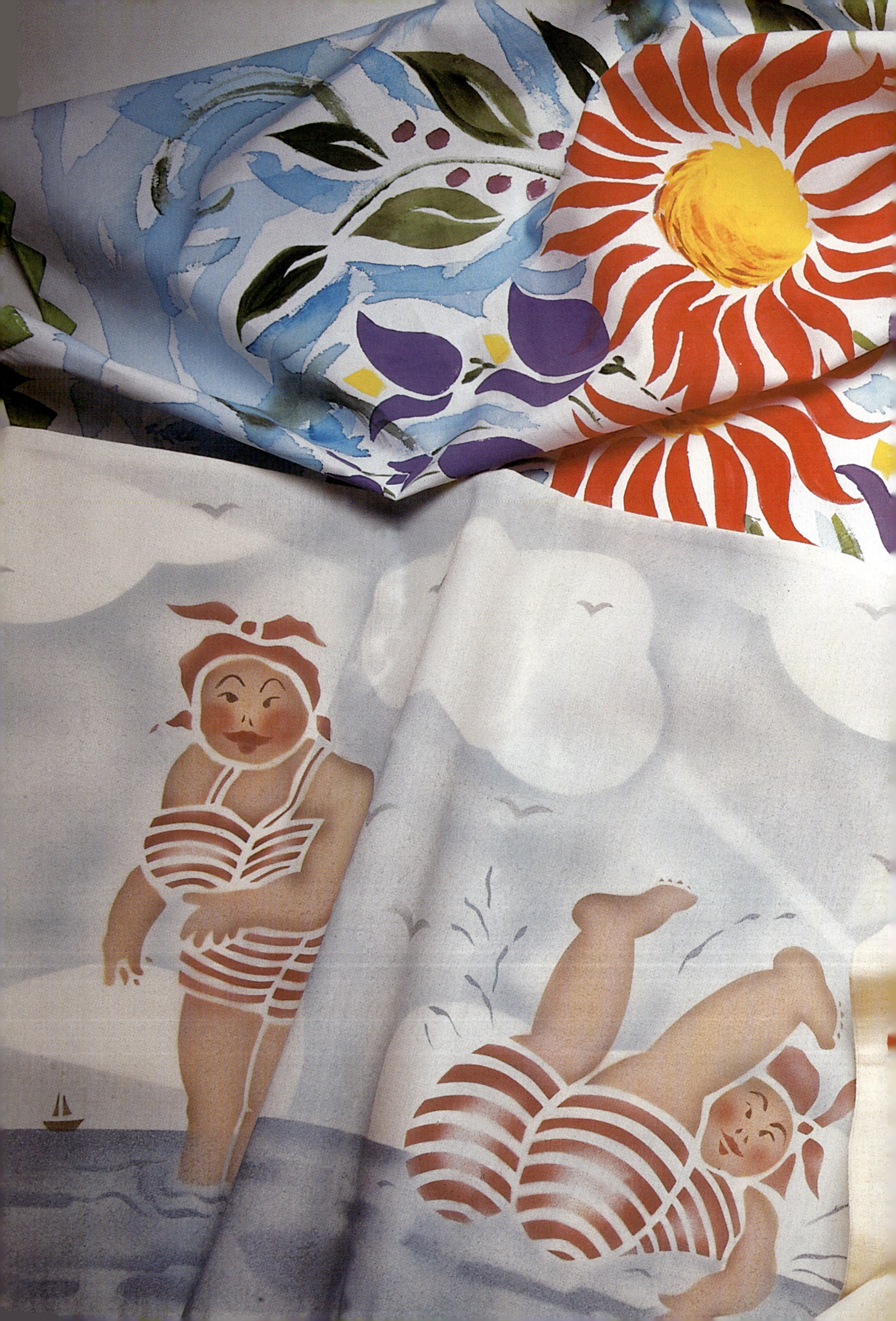

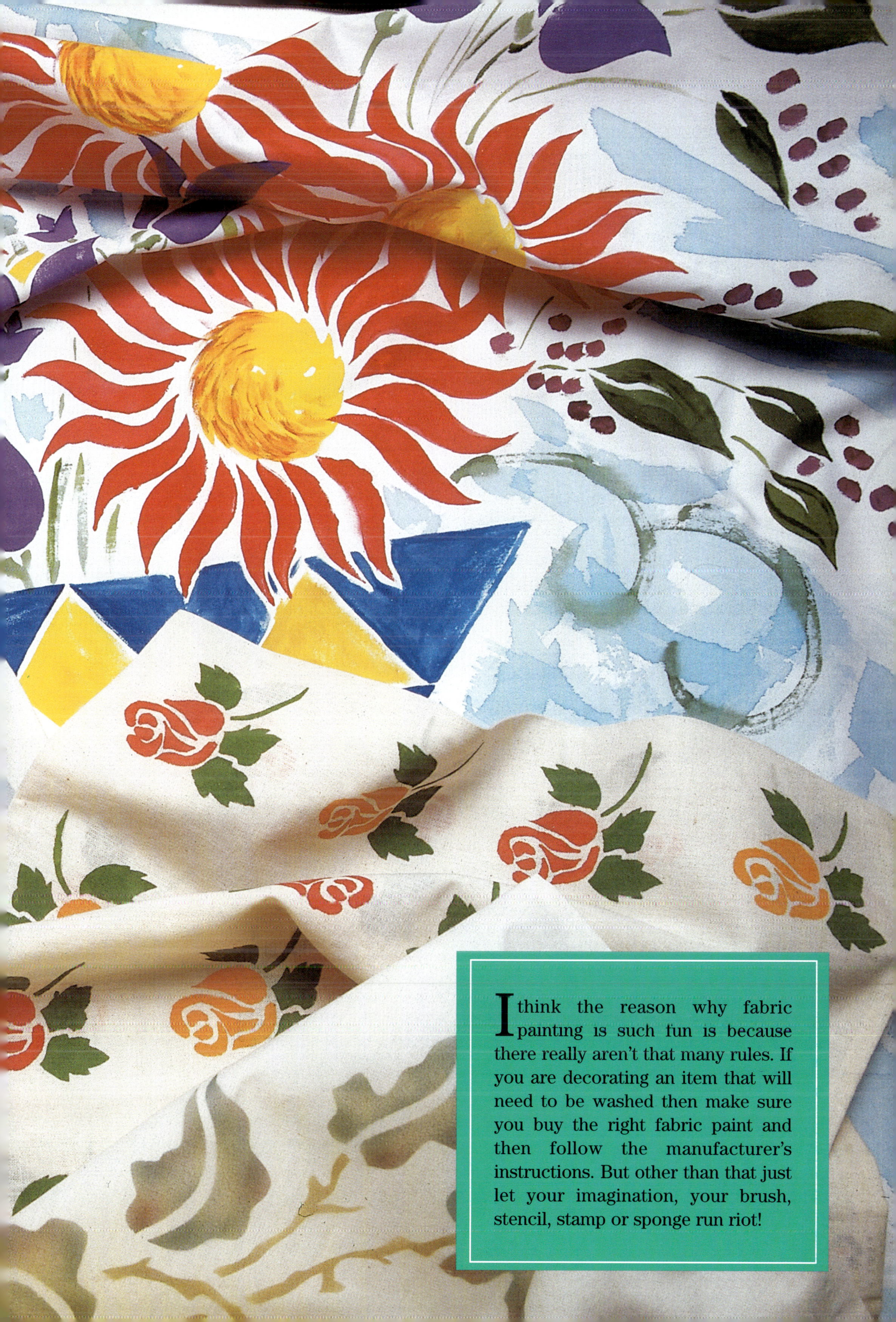

I think the reason why fabric painting is such fun is because there really aren't that many rules. If you are decorating an item that will need to be washed then make sure you buy the right fabric paint and then follow the manufacturer's instructions. But other than that just let your imagination, your brush, stencil, stamp or sponge run riot!

TECHNIQUES

Colour often often speaks louder than technique with fabric painting and you can create some tremendous effects by being clever with it. Practise mixing your colours on a saucer. Blue and yellow will make green, blue and red will make purple and yellow and red will make orange.

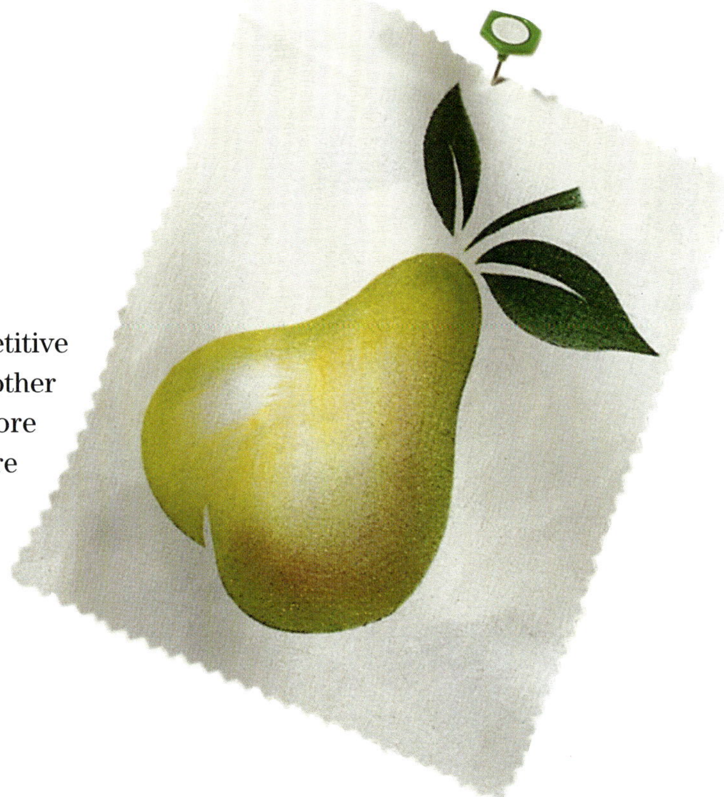

STENCILLING

Stencilling is a wonderful way to build up a repetitive pattern on fabric. You can over-stencil too adding other shapes in different colours to create a more complicated design. Stencilling allows for more intricate patterns while not demanding that the artist be fastidiously steady handed.

STAMPING

Whether it's memories of cutting out potato stamps at school or just that I'm naturally heavy handed, but I like to use stamping to achieve bold clear shapes and patterns. There is something reassuring about leaving a solid coloured imprint as you lift the stamp away from the fabric.

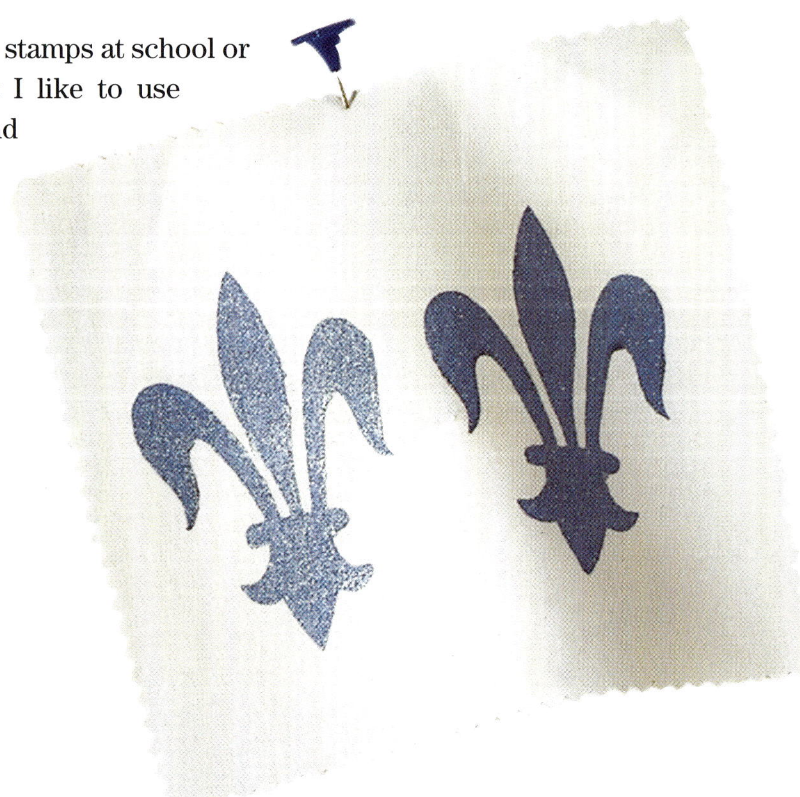

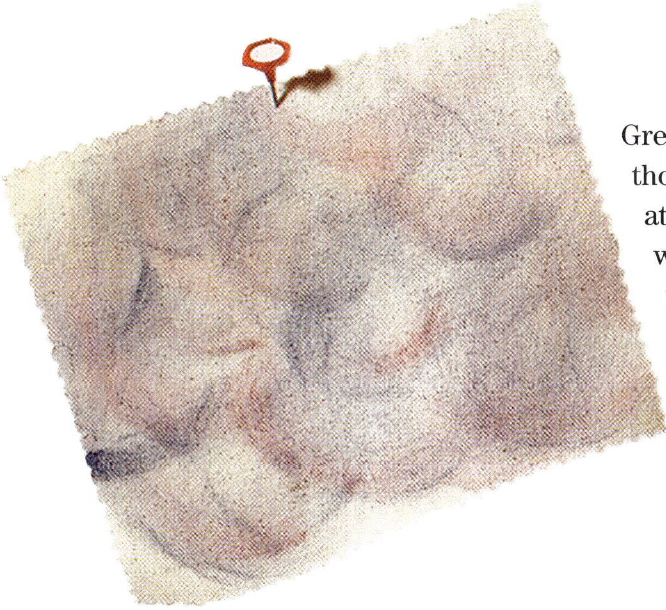

SPONGING

Great if you want to get the kids involved....it's pretty messy though so have plenty of newspaper and kitchen roll close at hand. This is a good way to cover large areas of fabric without painting on a block of colour. Sponging allows the weave of whatever textile you are painting to show through too.

FREEHAND

If you are artistic then treat your fabric just like a canvas and paint freestyle as you would normally. Freehand painting can be an incredibly effective way to interpret a design although it does need a bit of practice to get the right amount of paint on the brush. Use some tailor's chalk if you want to draw an outline first - or a faint pencil will do the job if the colour you are going to paint is dark.

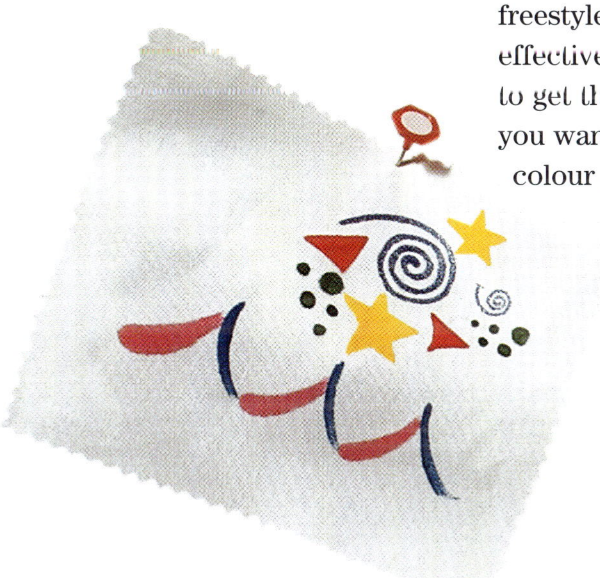

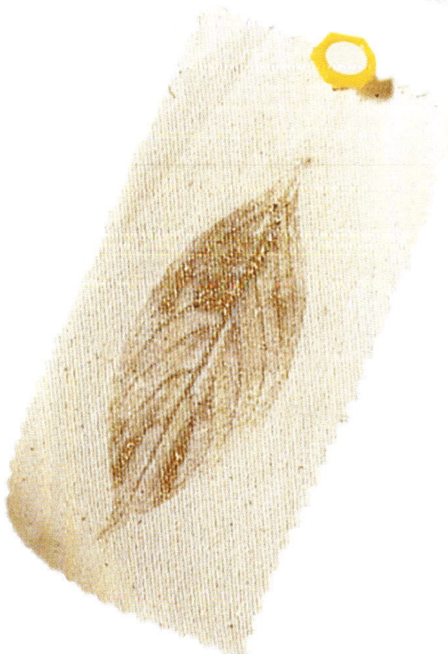

USE YOUR IMAGINATION

Because fabric painting is so versatile you can use just about anything to as tools of the trade or as sources of inspiration. I mentioned potatoes, well what about making imprints of autumn leaves, outlines of pressed flowers or trying the swirly effects of a feather dipped in your paint pot?

STEP-BY-STEP

Iron your fabric and lay on a flat surface protected by paper. If you are using a pattern trace it onto the stencil or sticky back rubber and cut out. Stick the rubber onto the piece of wood or perspex. Pour a small amount of paint into a saucer and go for it!

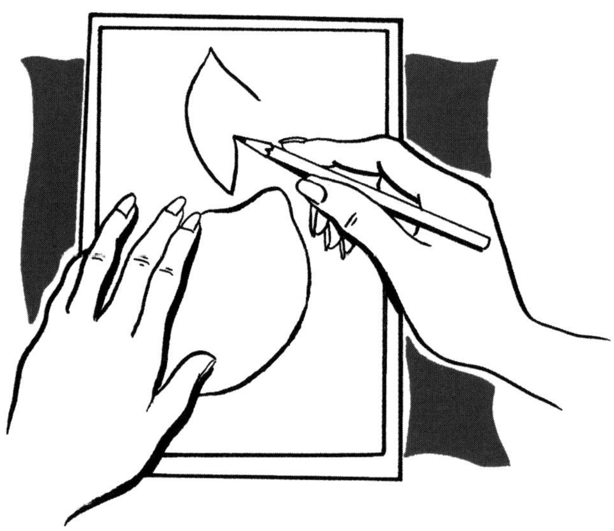

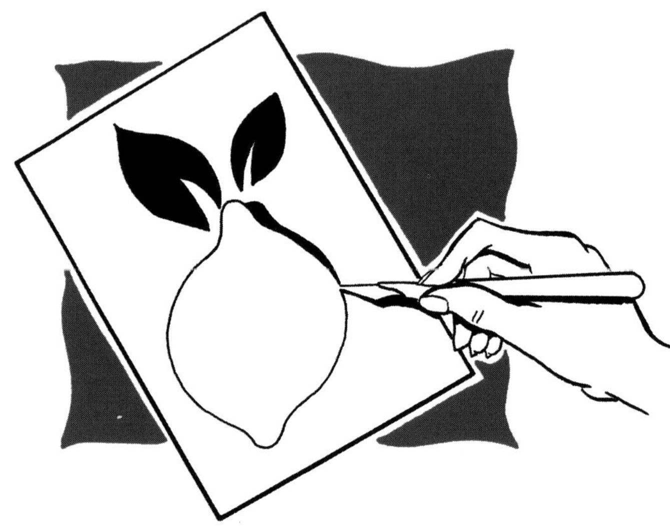

STENCILLING

Place your cut-out card in the chosen place on your fabric and smoothly paint or stipple with colour over the cut-out area. Peel it off gently away from you and before placing it down again make sure there are no smudges on the underside that might mark your fabric. You can always fill in missed places or even change the shape of the design with a brush.

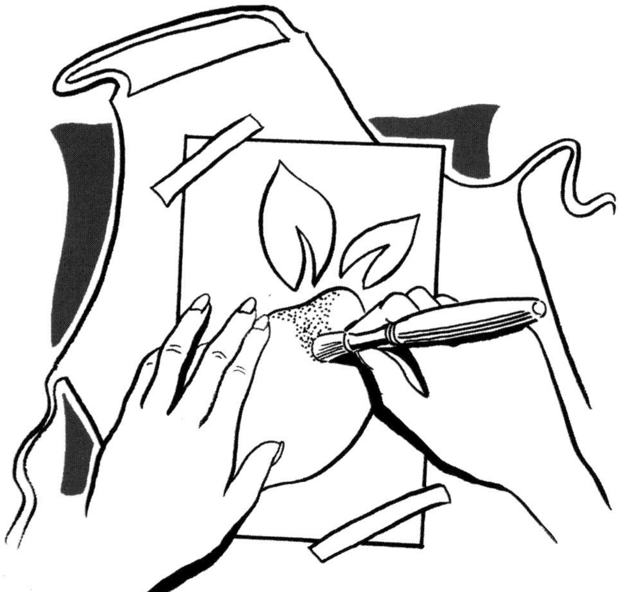

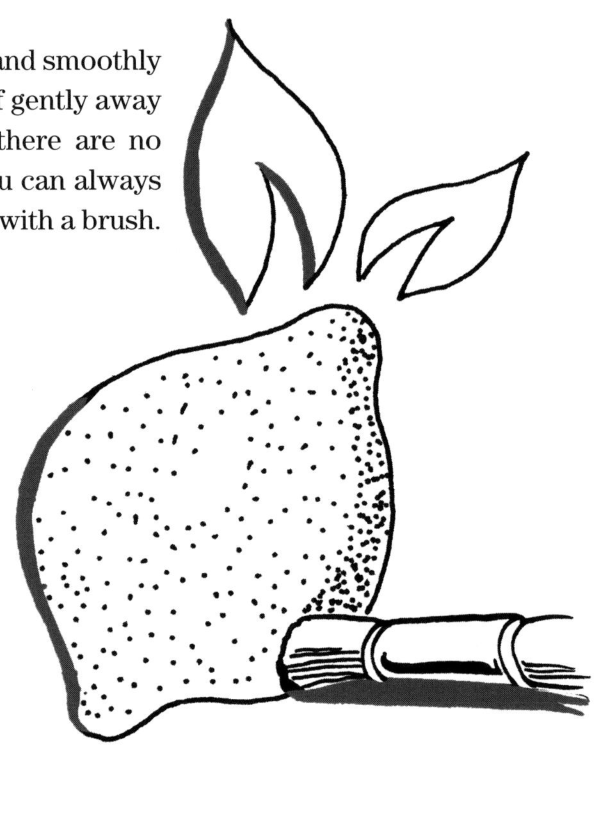

STAMPING

Gently press the rubber down into the paint and then lift. If it looks as though there are patches of the stamp with no paint on just paint some more on with your brush. (It's not cheating!)

Very carefully place the stamp on the fabric starting with the edge closest to you and press down firmly on top for a couple of seconds before equally gently lifting it off. Again fill in any patchy bits with your brush.

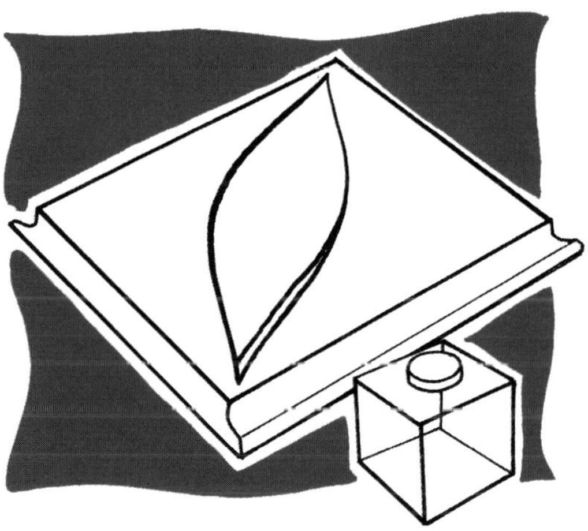

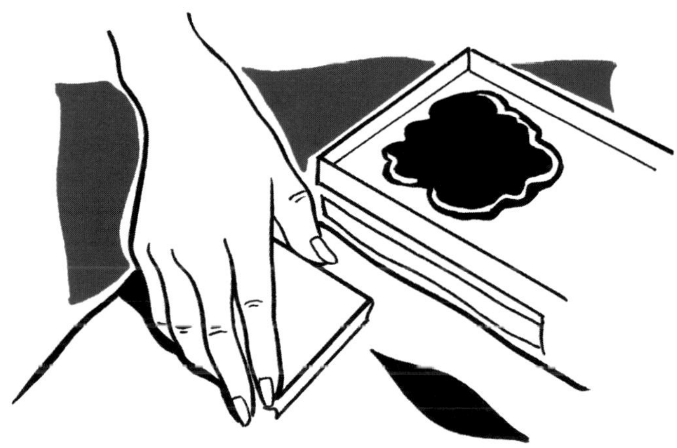

SPONGING

It's messy so clear the decks and mix up plenty of paint to complete whatever area you want to cover. It's a good idea to dilute the paint with water if you intend to sponge a background. Practise on a piece of paper.

FREEHAND

Just dip your brush in the paint pot, do a practice stroke on a piece of paper and start painting. If you don't feel confident to be fully artistic in a freestyle way then just use your brushstrokes to add emphasis or detail wherever your fabric painting needs a bit more welly!

FIXING

When you have finished fabric painting, most paints allow you to heat set your work by placing a sheet of paper between the iron and fabric and ironing it on cotton setting for five minutes on each side. It can then be washed gently in a mild detergent.

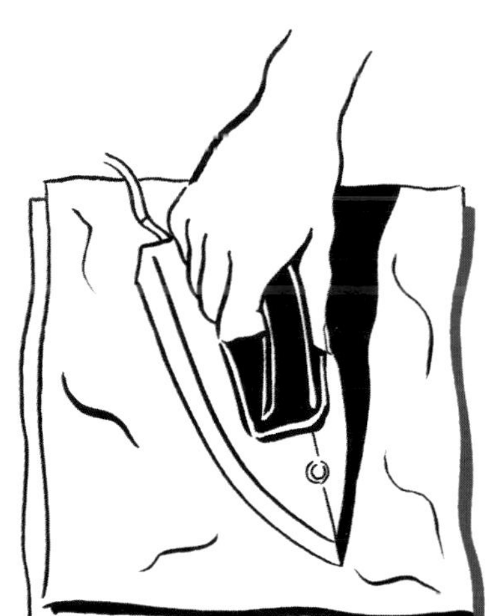

PATTERN

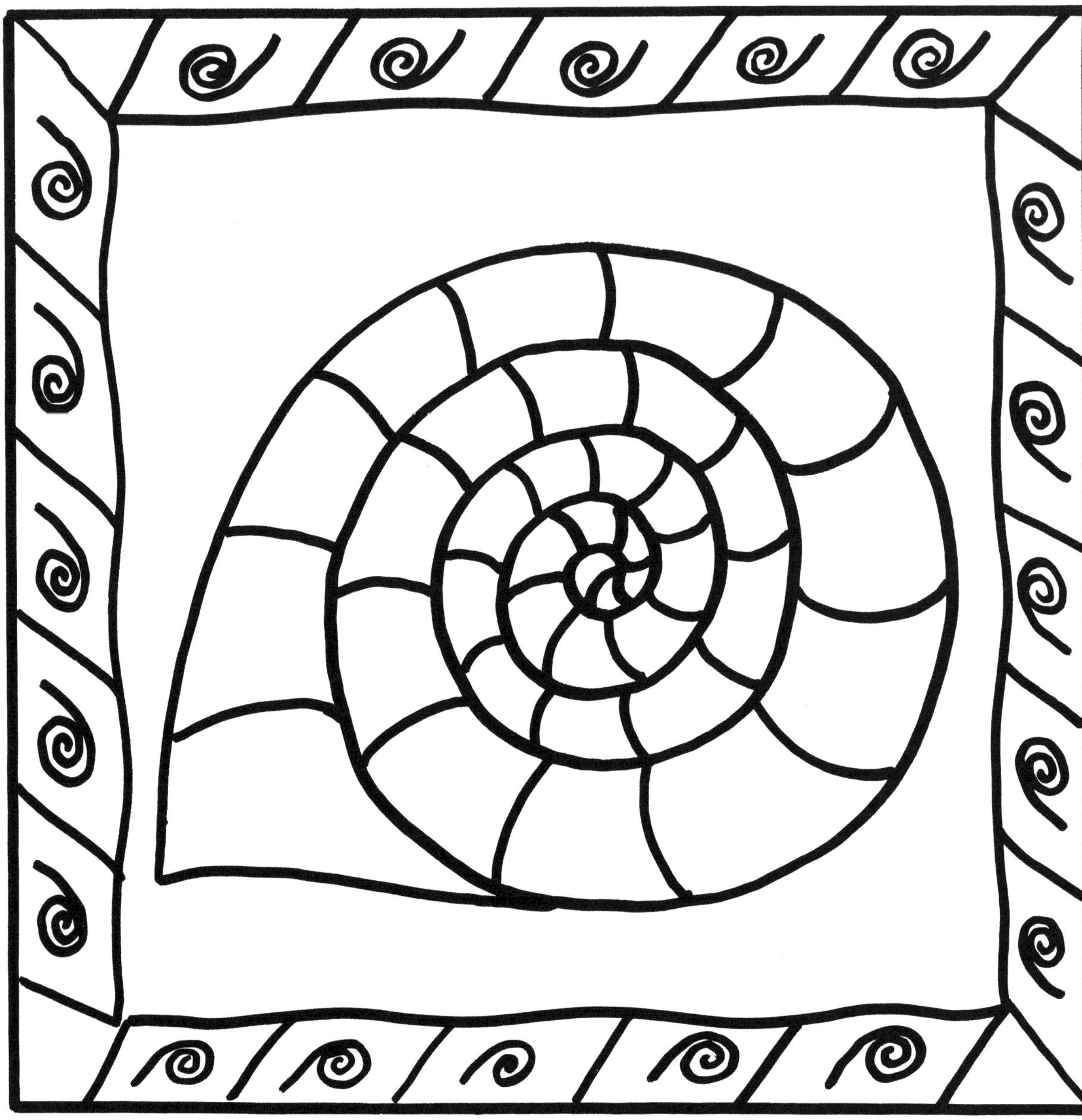

YOU WILL NEED

- A blank cushion cover
- Blue, green, gold and metallic purple fabric paints
- A big decorating brush for the base colour wash and smaller ones for painting the detail

FREESTYLE CUSHION COVER

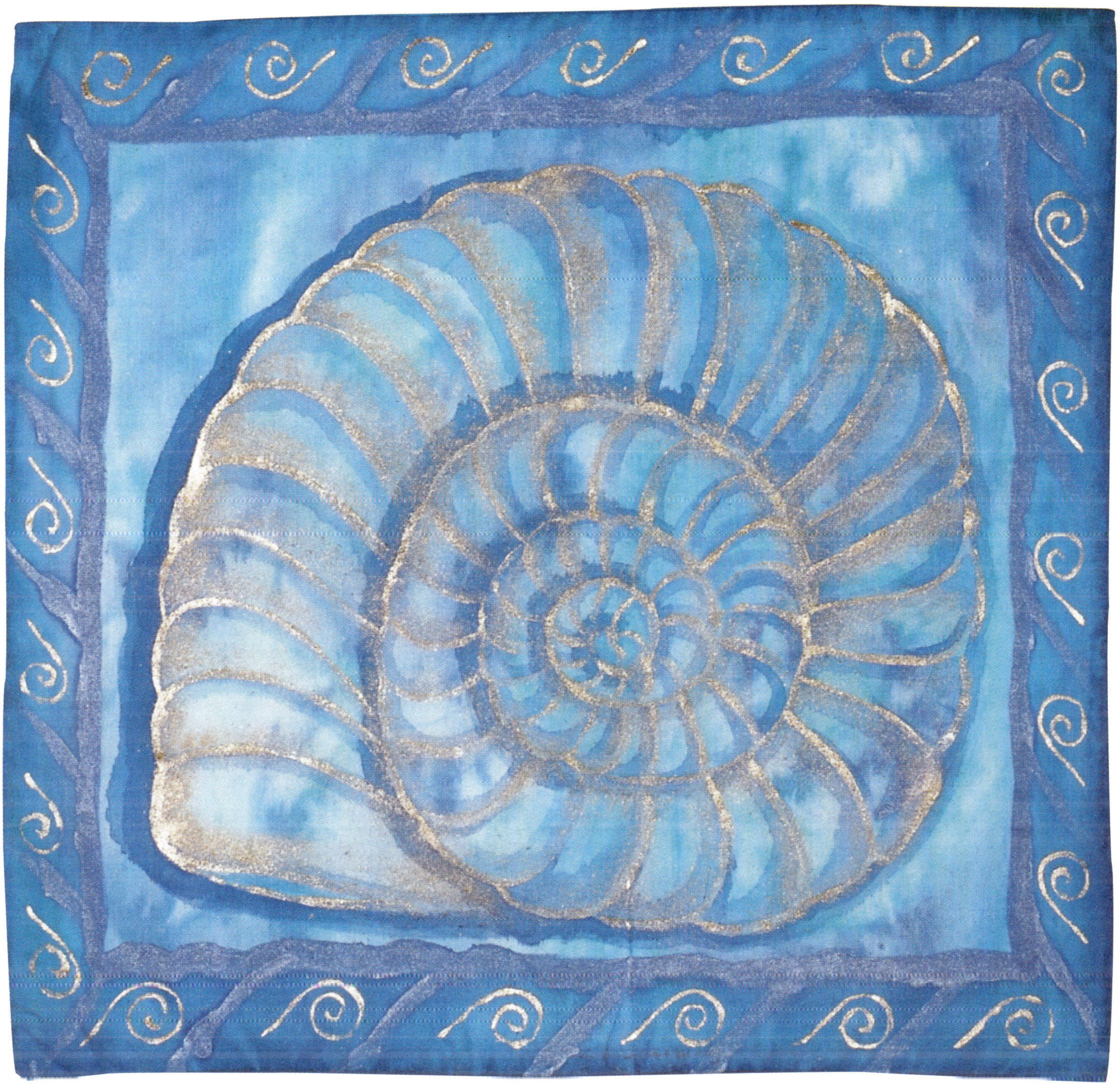

Sweep a watery blue and green wash over a blank cushion cover and let dry before adding swirly shell details in gold and undiluted blue and green.

PATTERN

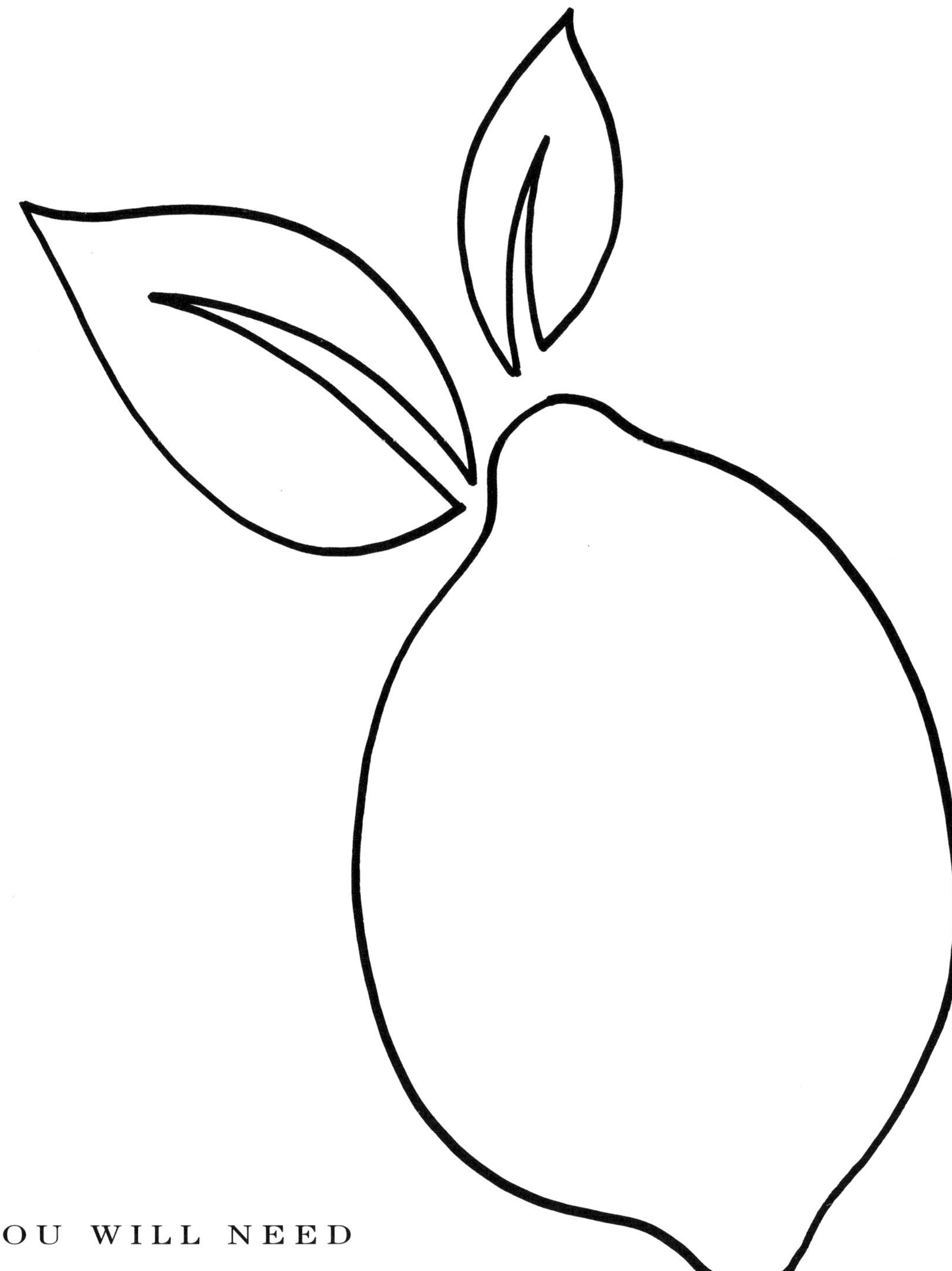

YOU WILL NEED

- A plain apron
- Yellow and green fabric paints
- Stencil card,
- Scalpel
- Stubby brush for stencilling
- Pencil

STENCILLED LEMON APRON

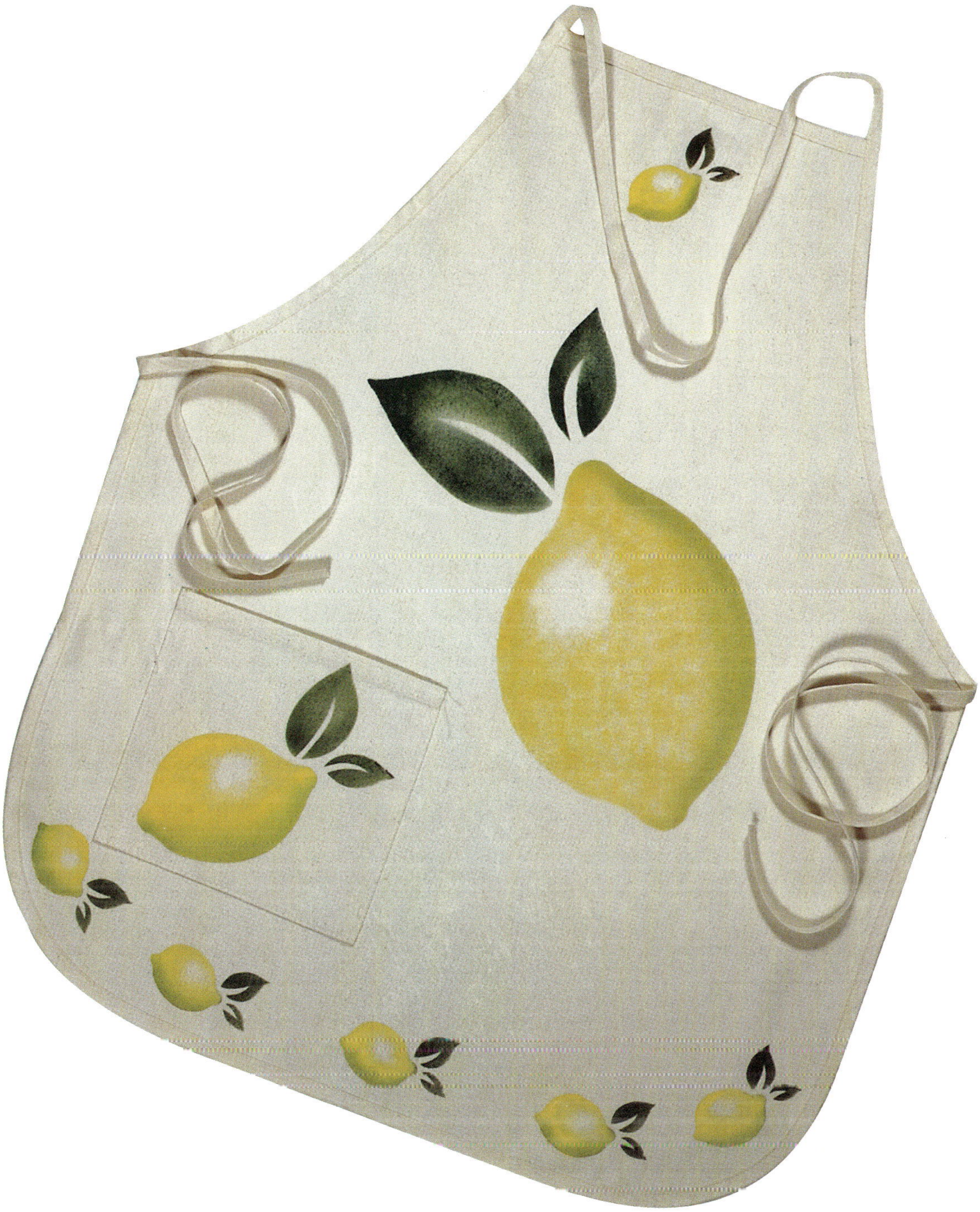

Enlarge or reduce this lemon pattern on a photocopier and cut out the shape from your stencil card before painting the design to add zest to a boring apron!

PATTERN

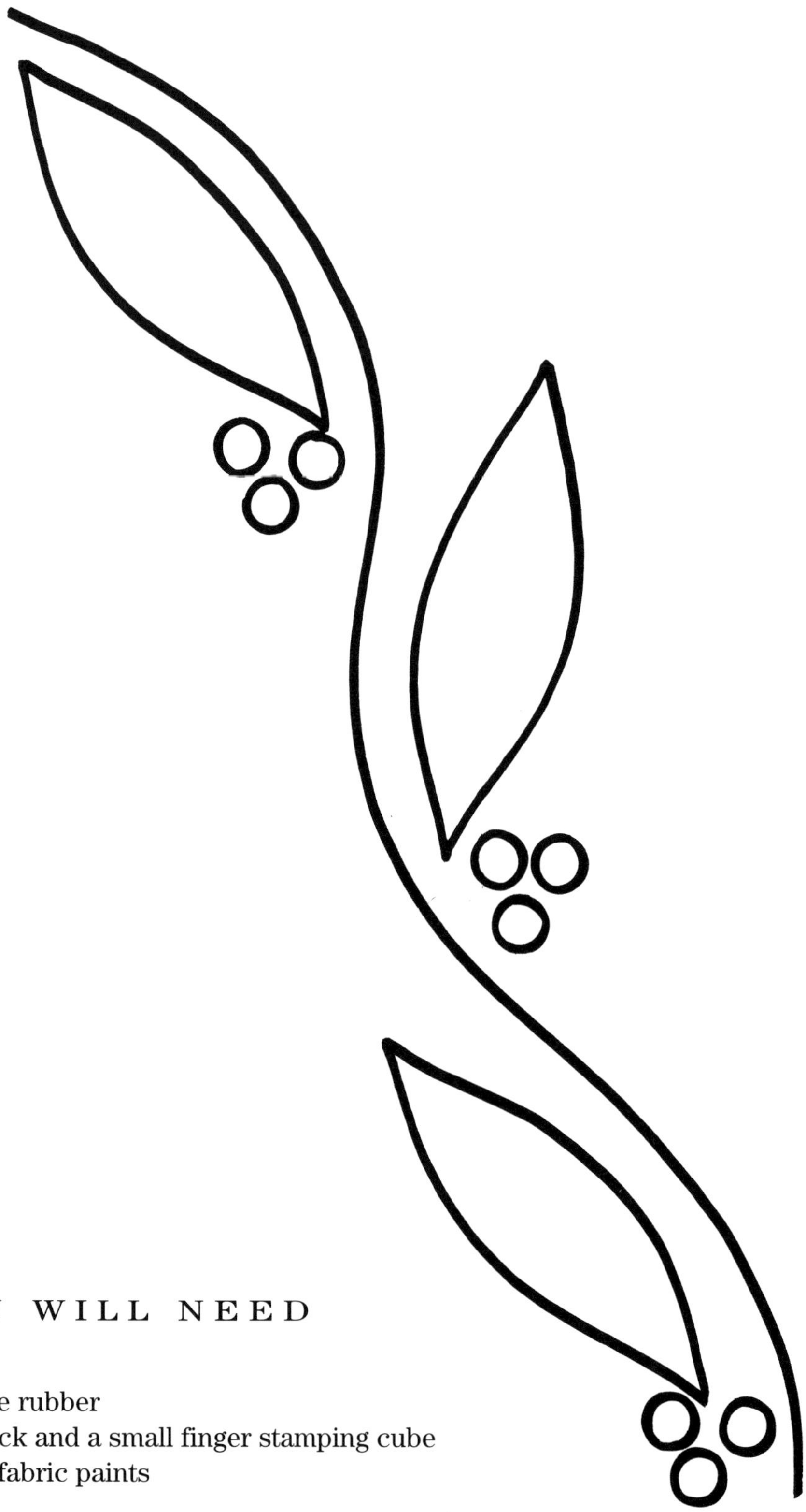

YOU WILL NEED

- Sticky back neoprene rubber
- A large stamping block and a small finger stamping cube
- Red, green and gold fabric paints
- Brushes
- Plastic trays or saucers

STAMPED NAPKIN

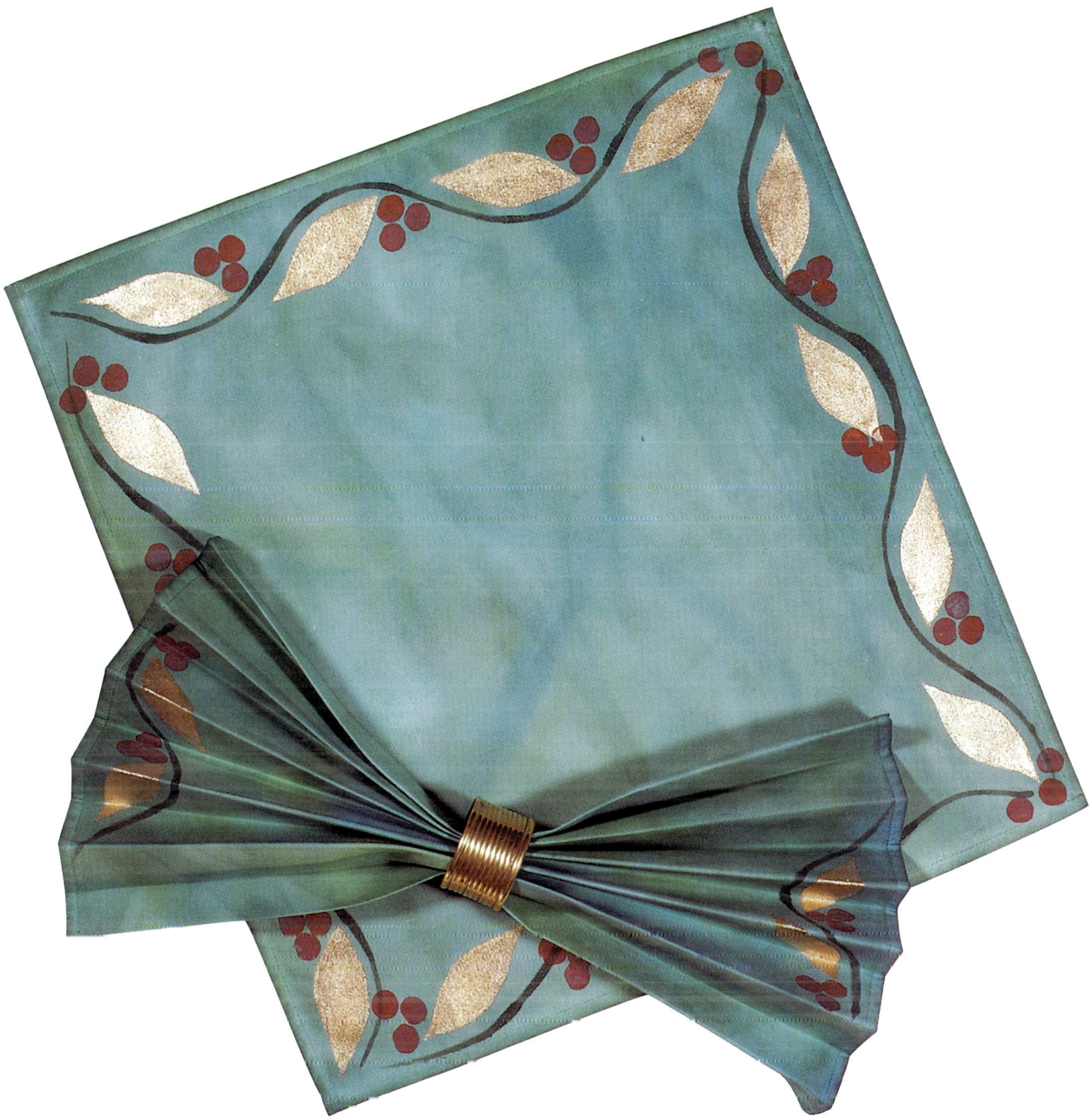

If you don't like the base colour of your plain napkins then apply a watery wash with a brush before adding detail with different stamps. Cut out the pattern shapes from the rubber and stick on the larger or smaller blocks and get stamping!

WHY STOP THERE?

As I've said before if it's fabric then you can paint it...here are some other ideas and items to inspire you.

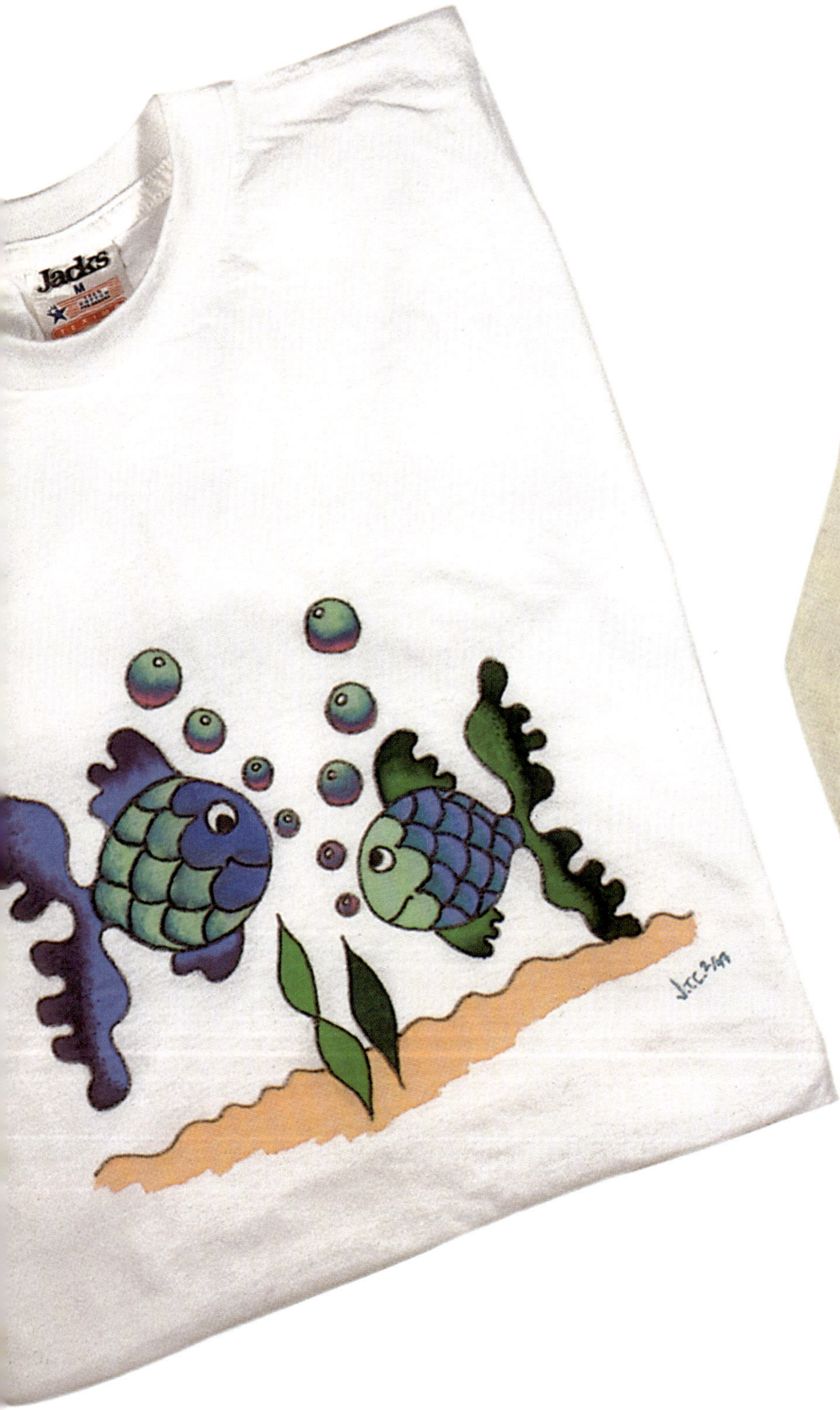

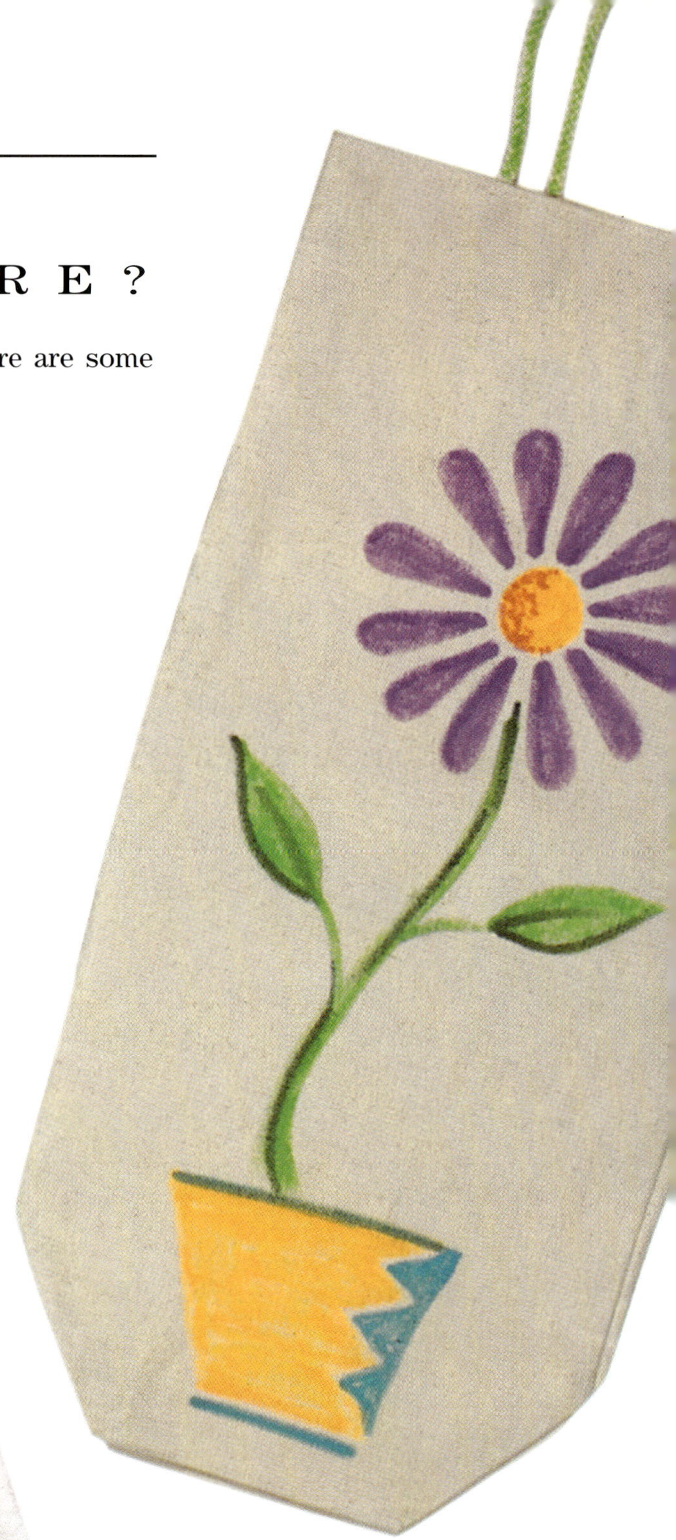

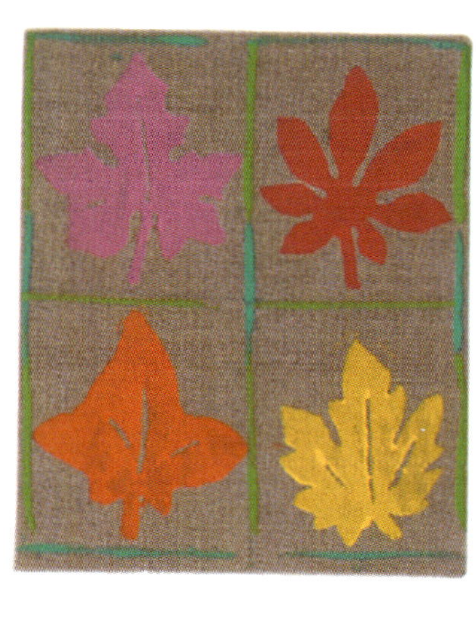

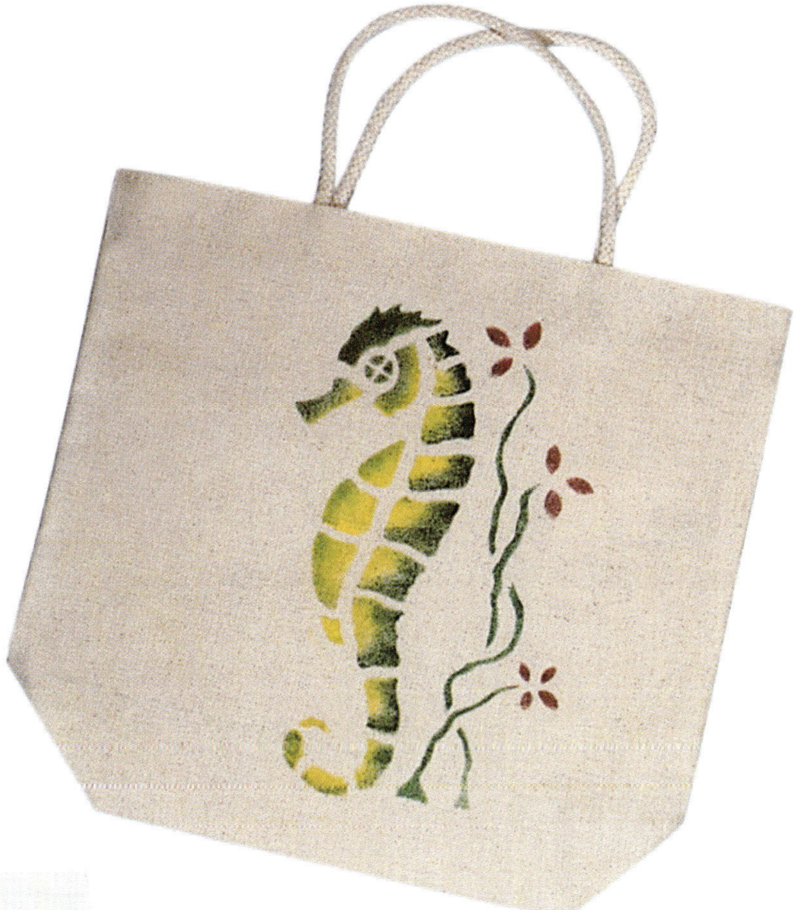

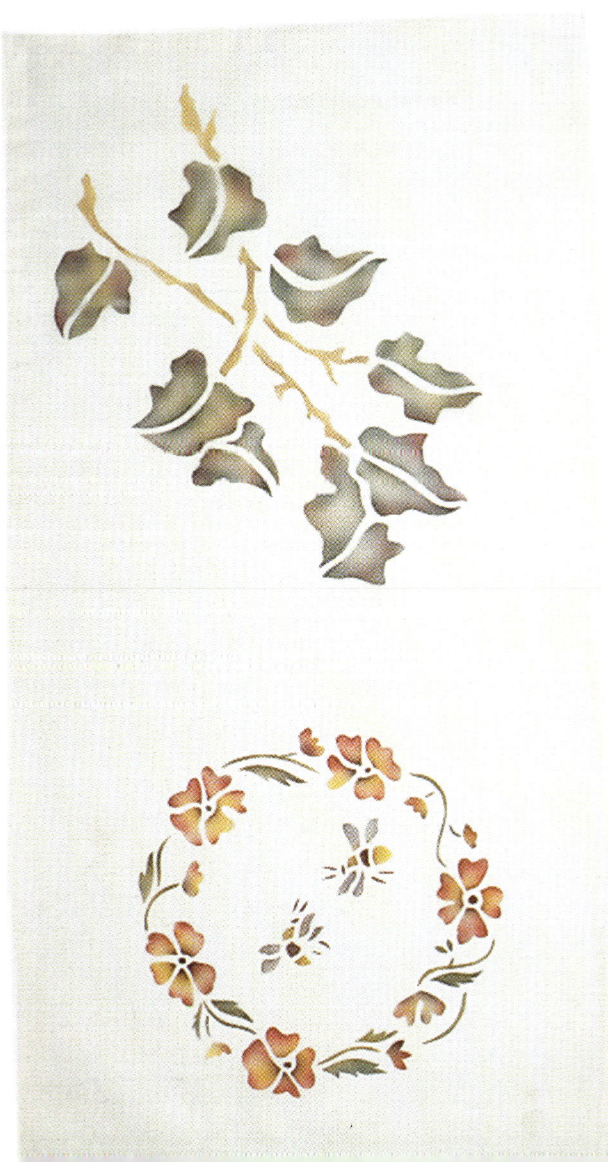

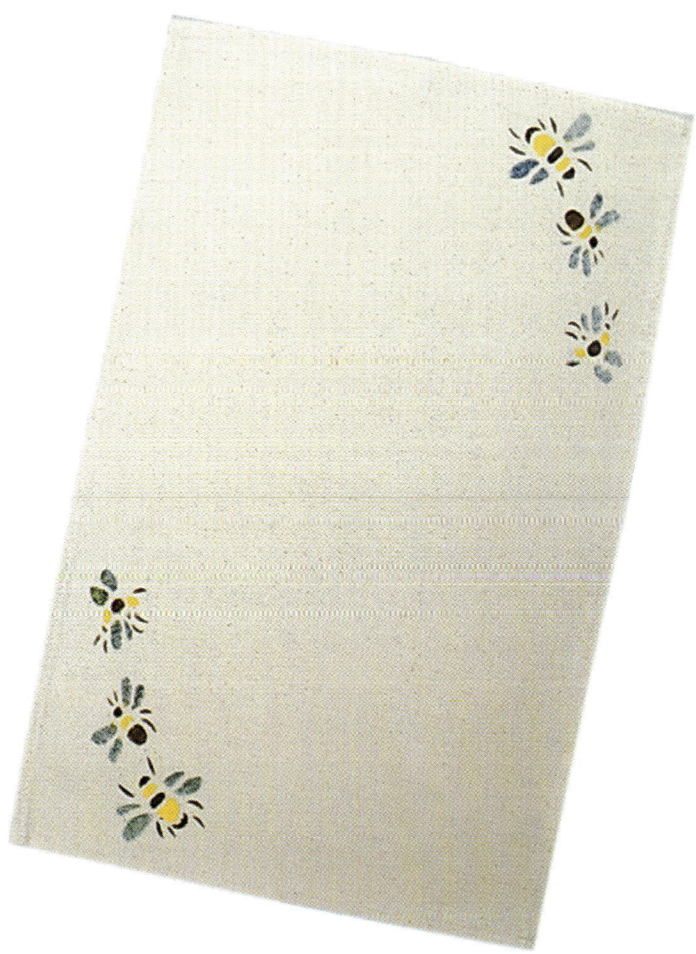

KITS

I have developed a range of kits complementary to this book. Each kit contains everything you will need and at the end you should have enjoyed creating a beautiful article.

Glass Painting: Practise these colourful designs onto acetate then paint them onto windows or mirrors to brighten up your home.

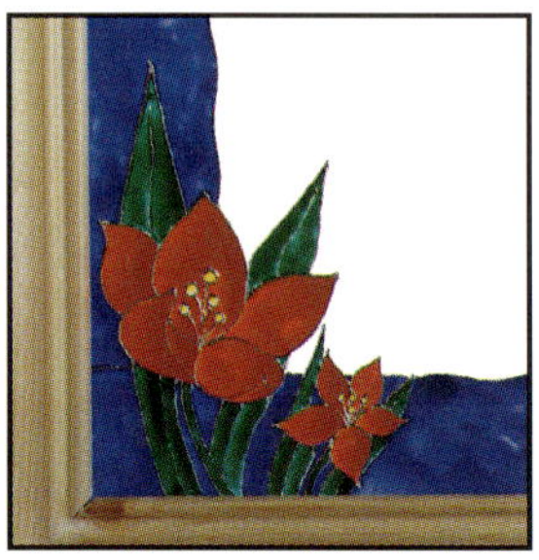

Contents:
- Liquid lead
- Varnish
- Acetate
- Glass paint
- Brushes
- Designs

Silk Painting: Silk scarves are beautiful as well as useful. It is a very satisfying craft so why not learn by doing this one and then do a design of your own?

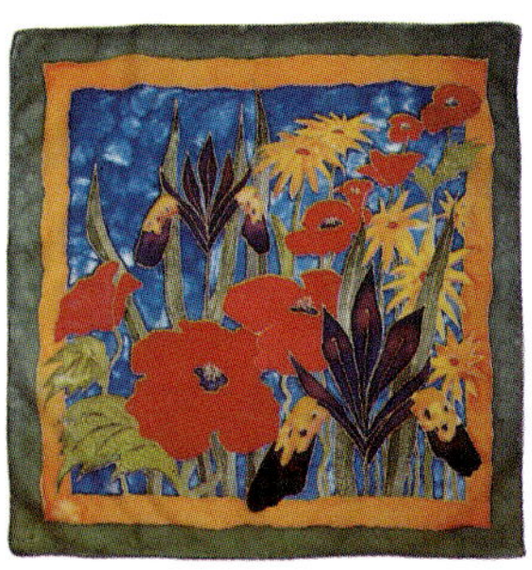

Contents:
- Gutta
- Silk
- Silk paints
- Pattern
- Brushes
- Tacks
- Pins
- Frame

Fabric Painting: Tablecloths, napkins, T-shirts, ties etc. all can be painted with your design. Try this tablecloth (or is it a wall-hanging!) and discover how to use stencils, stamps, sponging and special effects.

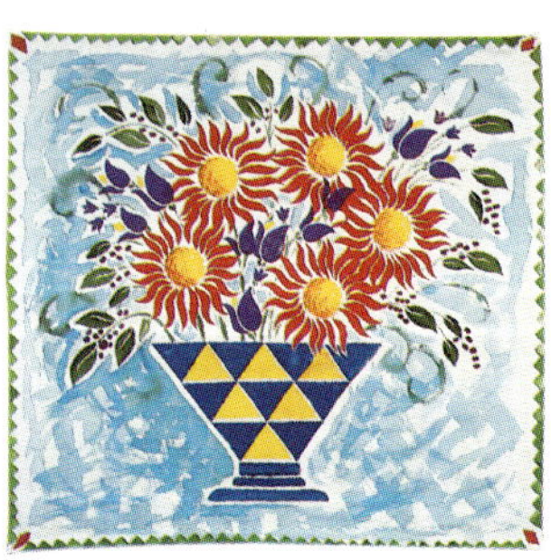

Contents:
- Tablecloth
- MDF block
- Fabric paints
- Scalpel
- Pattern
- Stencil card
- Sponge
- Brushes
- Neoprene rubber
- Perspex block

All the above are available from all good craft stores and by mail order from:

Really Vital Productions Ltd
PO Box 330
Slough SL2 3FH

Telephone orders call the orderline on 01753 648780

INDEX

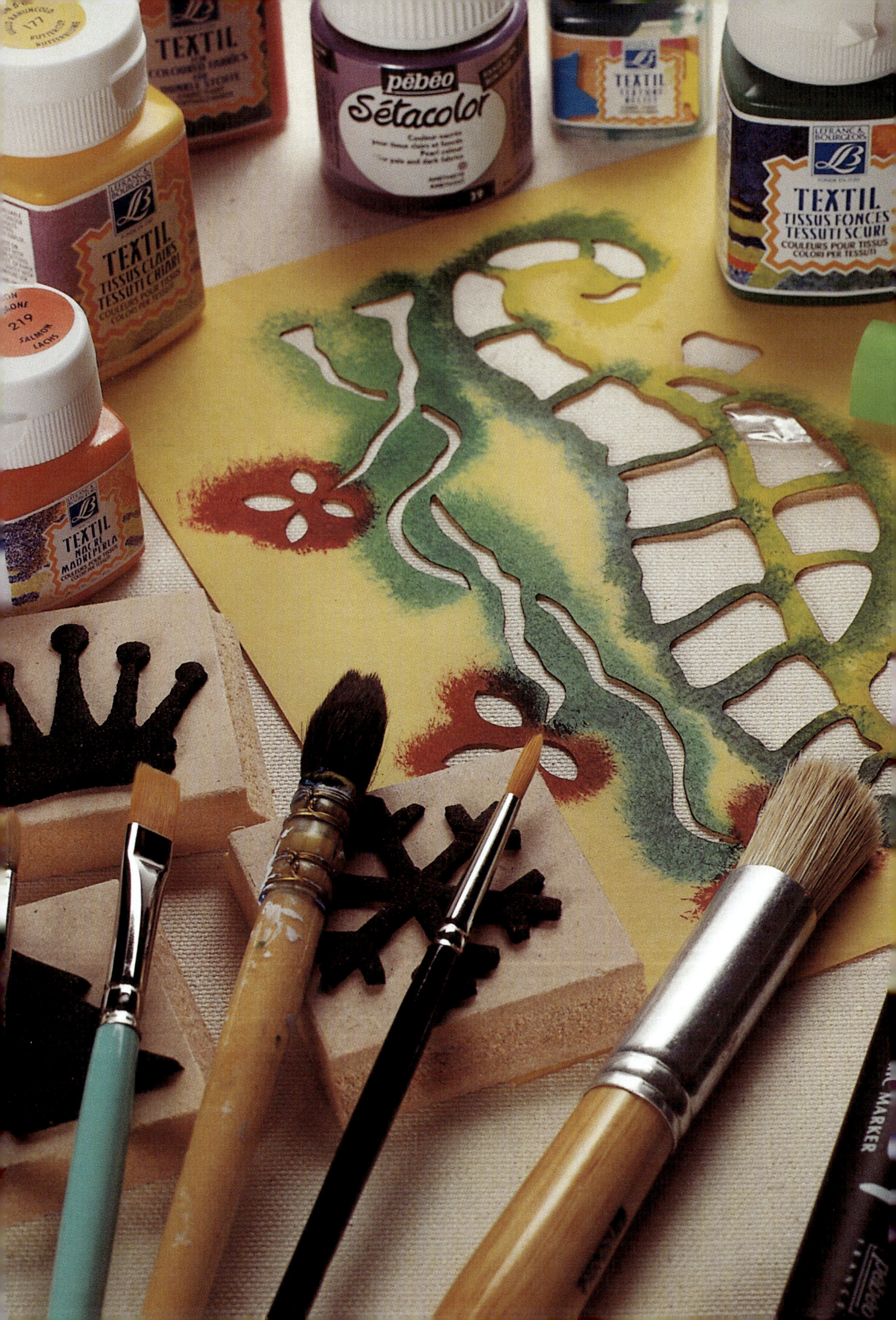

TEXTIL
pébéo
Sétacolor
TEXTIL
TISSUS FONCES
TESSUTI SCURI
COULEURS POUR TISSUS
COLORI PER TESSUTI
TEXTIL
TISSUS CLAIRS
TESSUTI CHIARI
219
SALMON
LACHS
TEXTIL
MARKER

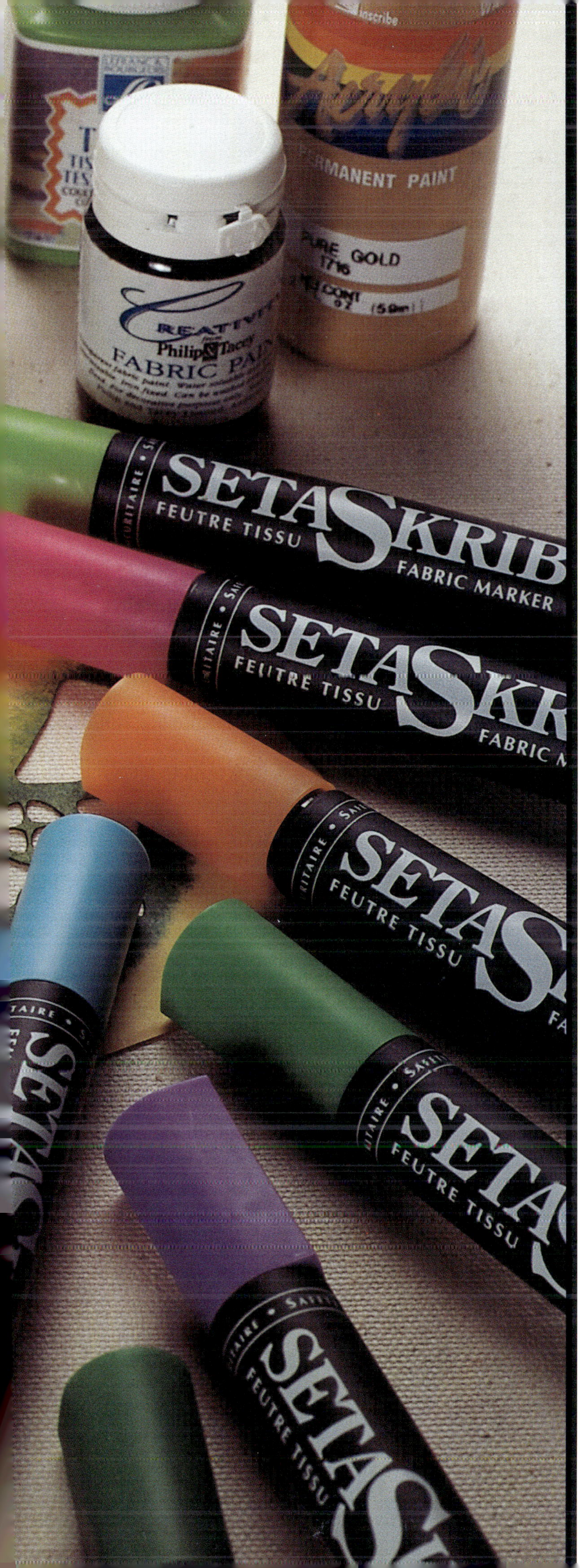

EQUIPMENT AND SUPPLIERS

It wasn't so long ago that anyone interested in craft had to scour the back of specialist magazines to find the mail order outlets that stocked the materials and components needed. Either that or you hoped that the local haberdashery department or artists' materials shop might have it in stock.

Things are very different today. While many high street shops now stock craft materials, we've also got several large craft shop chains both in town centres and in out of town shopping malls. These massive 'sheds' have got very extensive ranges of stock and are also extremely competitive pricewise which is good news for the shopper.

I'm a great browser and often set off to buy a couple of small items only to return home with the essentials to start a whole new craft.

New products are being developed all the time to make craft easier, from new paints and clays to bigger and more imaginative ranges of blanks to decorate and embellish.

Alongside all the products you will often find details of courses and workshops in your locality and one thing that seems to be universal to all suppliers, from the local art shop, to the mail-order girl on the end of the phone to the person on the check-out till in the craft 'shed' is a shared enthusiasm to help you and me get the most out of our craft.

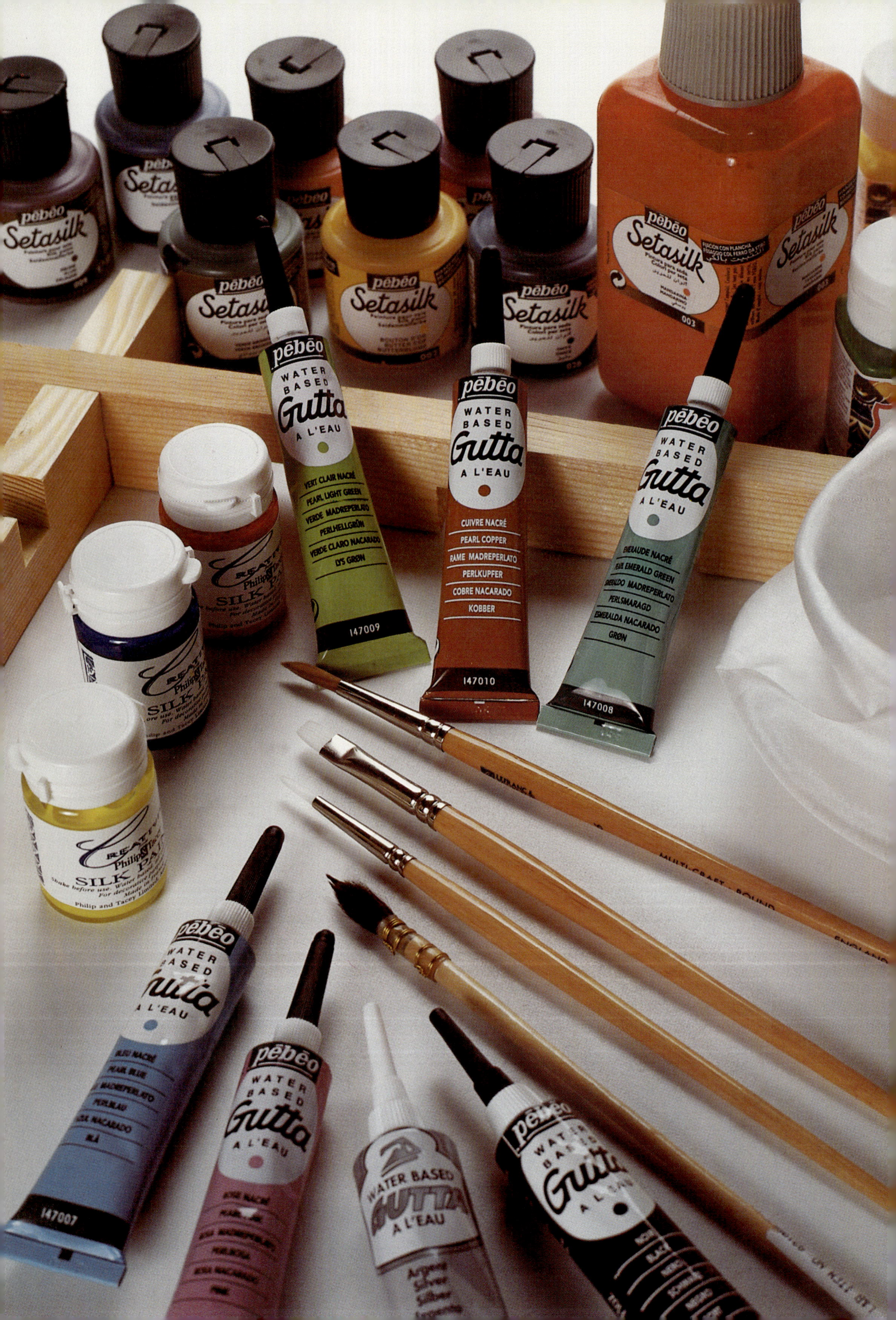
pébéo
Setasilk
WATER BASED
Gutta
A L'EAU
VERT CLAIR NACRÉ
PEARL LIGHT GREEN
VERDE MADREPERLATO
PERLHELLGRÜN
VERDE CLARO NACARADO
LYS GRØN
147009
CUIVRE NACRÉ
PEARL COPPER
RAME MADREPERLATO
PERLKUPFER
COBRE NACARADO
KOBBER
147010
EMERAUDE NACRÉ
PEARL EMERALD GREEN
PERLSMARAGD
ESMERALDA NACARADO
GRØN
147008
147007
WATER BASED
GUTTA
A L'EAU
SILK PAINT
Philip and Tacey

SUPPLIERS

Manufacturers, Importers and Wholesalers

Atlascraft
4 Plumtree St
The Lace Market
Nottingham
NG1 1JL
For your local suppliers please call customer services :
Tel: 0115 9415280
Fax: 0115 9415281

A wide range of products covering most crafts. Main importers of Deka paints. Their range is available at John Lewis Partnership Shops and on mail order from:

Cats Group
PO Box 12
Saxmundham
Suffolk
Tel: 01728 648717

ColArt Fine Art & Graphics Ltd
Whitefriars Avenue
Harrow
Middlesex
HA3 5RH
For your local suppliers please call customer services:
Tel 0181 427 4343
Fax: 0181 863 7177

A large portfolio of well-known branded fine art materials including Winsor & Newton, Lefranc & Bourgeois and Dryad.

Daler Rowney Ltd
P.O.Box 10
Bracknell
Berkshire
RG12 8ST
For your local suppliers please call customer services :
Tel: 01344 424621
Fax: 01344 486511

Largest manufacturer of a fully comprehensive range of colours, brushes, surfaces and artists and craft accessories

Philip & Tacey Ltd
North Way
Andover
Hampshire
SP10 5BA
For your local suppliers please call customer services :
Tel: 01264 332171
Fax: 01264 332226
E-Mail: sales@philipandtacey.co.uk

One of the longest established family firms in the arts and craft business. They carry a large range of stock and are the importers of the well-known Pebeo range of paints.

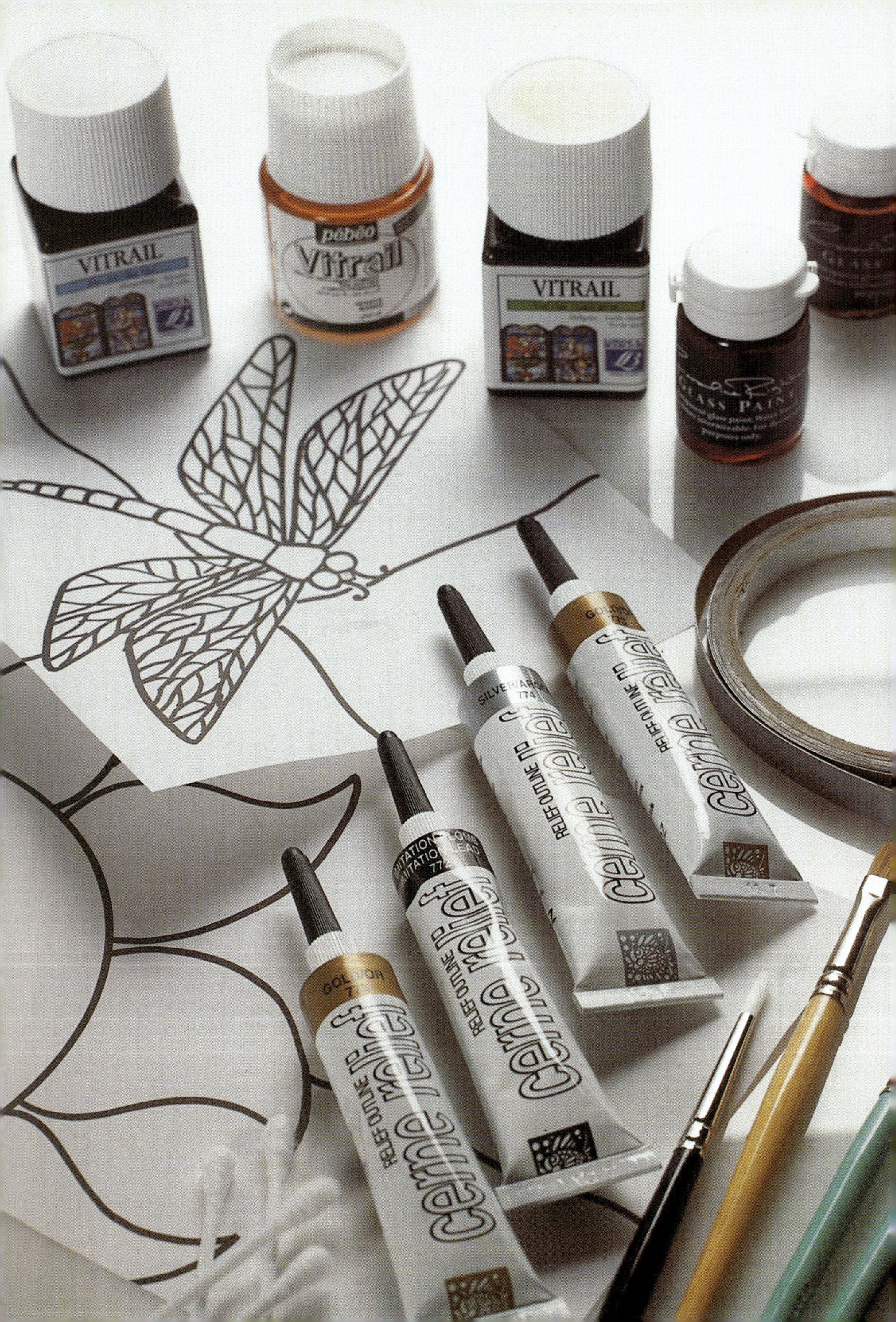
VITRAIL
pébéo
Vitrail
VITRAIL
GLASS PAINT
cerne relief
RELIEF OUTLINE
GOLD/OR
SILVER/ARGENT
774
IMITATION LEAD
772

SUPPLIERS

Retail, Mail Order and Training Workshops

Creative World
The Bishop Centre
Bath Rd
Taplow
Berkshire
SL6 0NY
Tel: 01628 661331
and at

Creative World
The Galleries
Bristol
Tel: 0117 929 7775

These are one of the new expanding chains of larger shops. They carry thousands of lines covering all crafts. Good for browsing!

The Dwelling Ltd
76 Park St
Camberley
Surrey
GU15 3PT
Tel: 01276 63255
Fax: 01276 63233
Free Phone Order Line 0800 854882

Stencilling, mural and paint effects specialists. A very helpful and efficient mail order service

Mulberry Craft
Cherry Tree House
7 Dean St
Marlow
Bucks
Tel 01628 487900
Fax: 01628 475810
E-Mail: Mulberrycraft@BTInternet.com

Retail workshop and mail order, offer an extensive range of supplies both retail and mail order. Chris Thompson and her team are always willing to give friendly advice and also offer training courses and workshops.

George Weil & Sons
The Wharehouse
Reading Arch Road
Redhill
RH1 1HG
Tel: 01737 778868
Fax: 01737 778894

A good general supplier who are known for their importing of the extensive Arty's cotton, silk and gutta collection and offer a full mail order service.

Nexus presents "Create It .....In an Evening", a series of books developed by Caroline Righton (your regular columnist on *Popular Crafts* TV presenter, producer, journalist and craft specialist), in response to the growing demand for innovative craft books suitable for today's busy lifestyle.

Other titles in this series

If you have enjoyed making the projects in this book, why not try your hand at other crafts? Other titles in this series include:

Create it with Paper in an Evening — Nine projects for making things with paper - découpage, papier mâché and hand-made paper. All are easily achievable by beginners with simple illustrated instructions and full colour throughout.

ISBN 1-85486-175-1

Create it with Wax, Clay & Plaster in an Evening — Another nine easy to make projects using wax, clay and plaster. Again split into three sections each one comprising an introduction, equipment list, techniques and a step-by-step guide to the basic skills needed.

ISBN 1-85486-177-8

Create it with Thread in an Evening — In this book Caroline offers the option of applying your skills to three different mediums: quilting, appliqué and cross-stitch. All the projects are easily achievable by beginnners and great fun for all skill levels.

ISBN 1-85486-176-X

All the above titles should be obtainable from good bookshops. In the event of difficulty please contact the Books Division, Nexus Special Interests Ltd., Nexus House, Boundary Way, Hemel Hempstead, Herts HP2 7ST Tel: 01442 266551

NEW TITLE FROM NEXUS SPECIAL INTERESTS

Alice and Daisy: Edwardian rag doll sisters to make and dress
Valerie Janitch

The basic Alice & Daisy dolls are simple enough for a beginner to make and equally easy to dress, with charming colour photographs that follow Alice & Daisy through their busy social diary. Whether it's lessons, shopping, tea in the country, a birthday party or just retiring to bed, an appropriate outfit is a necessity (plus beribboned underpinnings, of course!). Be warned! Once you have made the fashion conscious rag dolls, they won't allow you to resist the temptation to make their entire wardrobe. This book gives you the instructions to make the pretty and romantic Edwardian fashions that are such an important part of their sophisticated lifestyle. Alice & Daisy may be rag dolls, but *mere* rag dolls they are not!

To be published Autumn 1998. ISBN 1-85486-183-2

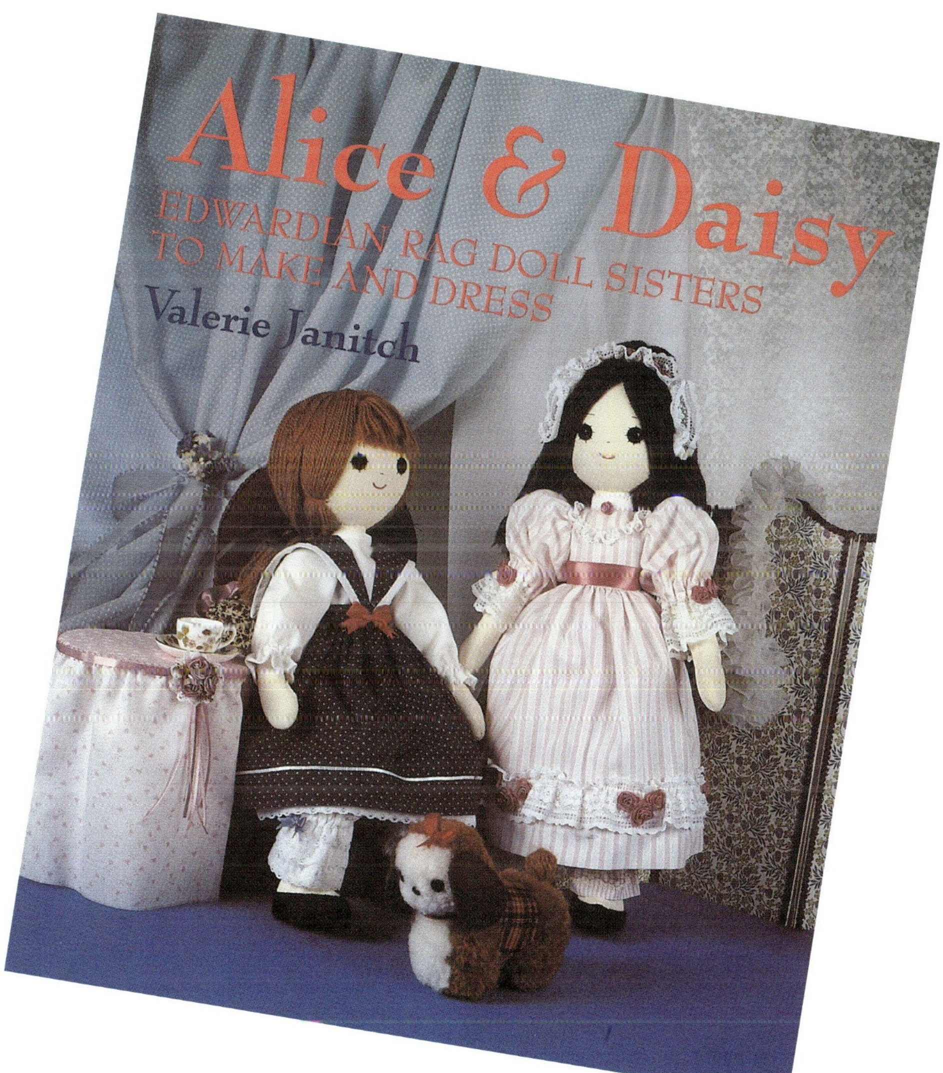

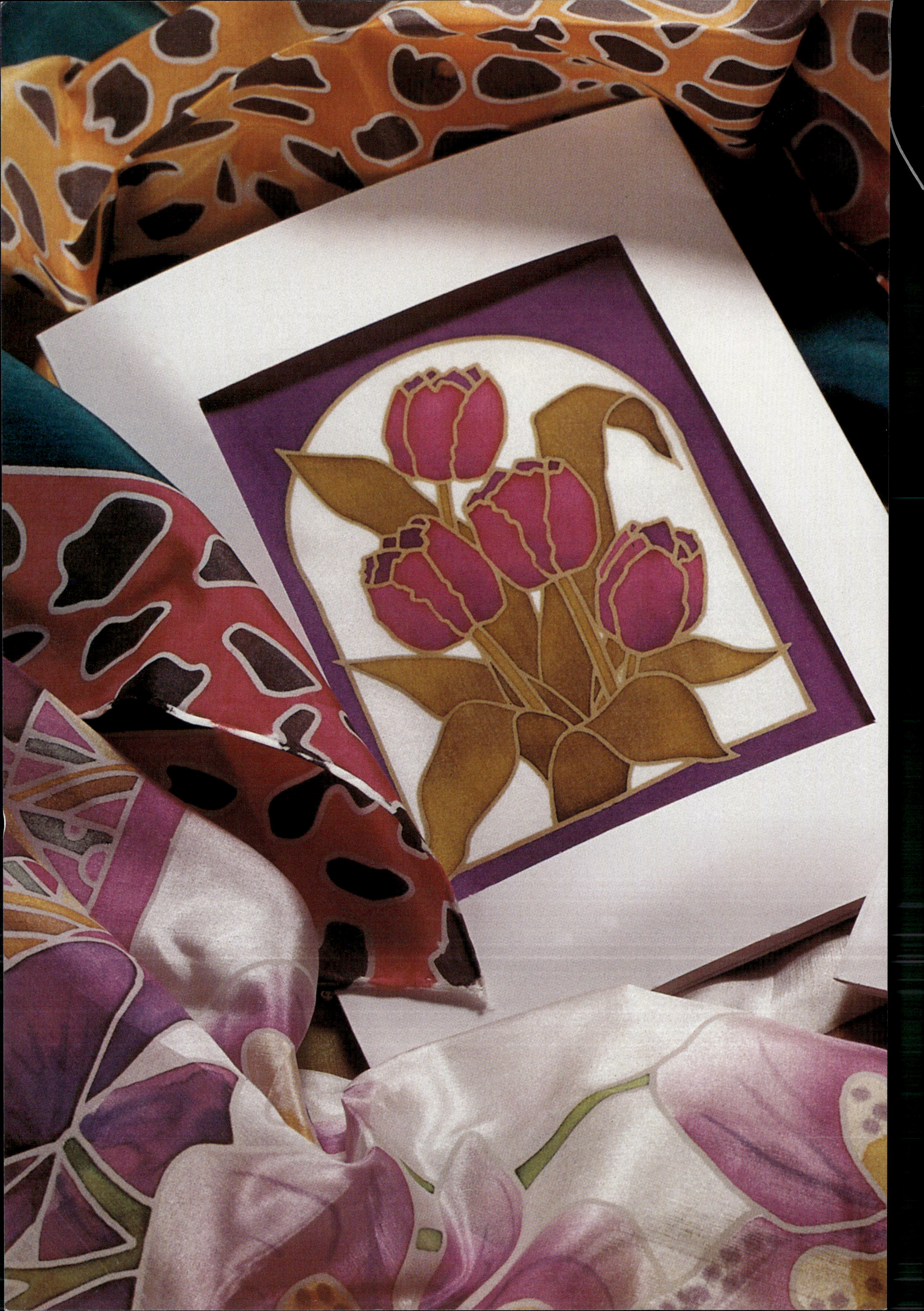